United Stat
Freedom vs. Communism –
The Last Stand for America's Families

James Scarangella

Copyright © 2024

All Rights Reserved

Dedication

Life is a culmination of influences, and to all of them that made me up, I am grateful... both good and bad. Among the most significant influences in my life have been my parents, family, and friends.

To my wife and children, you have all provided different insights at different times to help forge a grounded perspective from which to appreciate the true wonder and specialness of this life. Even with its drudgery and pain, life is beautiful, and we have been blessed. Thank you.

To all the moms and dads who are struggling to raise their families, I hope this book helps you understand what immoral forces you are really up against.

Acknowledgment

To the extent anything sounds familiar, it should be attributed to the fact that I am constantly seeking input from many respected people. To begin with, the universe of modern conservatism with emphasis on the late and great Rush Limbaugh, a true beacon of truth and understanding. Other positive influences and influencers include the Jesuits at Fordham, Ronald Regan, Donald Trump, Newt Gingrich, Glenn Beck, Elon Musk, Bill O'Reilly, and now Jesse Kelly, a true beacon of light.

To the extent my pragmatic work sounds like them, well, it is because they are all unique, insightful, and truthful, and my gratitude goes out to them. There are, of course, many more tangential influences like Wikipedia and various Duck Duck Go Searches but suffice it to say that I am a pragmatic "life sponge" and love to take in as many angles as possible.

To the negative influences and my partial motivation for writing this, they too must be acknowledged: Covid and the new era of tyranny, the Obamas, the Clintons, Pelosi, Gore, Adam Schiff, Bill Gates, Pol Pot, Mark Zuckerberg, George Soros, Bill Ayers, Joseph Stalin, Mao Tse Tung, and any corporate fascist tied to any government bureaucrat that seeks division through misinformation and/or repression of people, in order to subjugate and control us, and stifle the human spirit… thank you, you "woke" me up and hopefully, I can wake others.

About the Author

James Scarangella is a working-class father of 5 who combines economic life lessons with business experiences, teaching experiences, family, history, and community in an attempt to show how we can identify with one or more areas and help stabilize our country and propel it forward and away from Communism. As a father of 3 girls and 2 boys, with a BA and MA from Fordham University in Economics, teaching certifications from NY State, Army reserve experience and solid corporate experience with some of the largest corporations on the planet for over 30 years, James seeks to combine this eclectic background for a common purpose in America 12.0.

Growing up in the Bronx and born into a solid, union-supporting Democratic "pre-Regan" family, life was socially bright. His father worked in the union as an airline mechanic for Pan Am, while his mother held a job as a bookkeeper. He lived in a modest semi-attached row home and had a friend-filled childhood.

Back in the late 70s and early 80s, the Bronx was buzzing with activity, both good and bad. Kids from all different backgrounds - Black, White, Jewish, Italian, Polish, Venezuelan, Puerto Rican, Irish, Chinese - are a true melting pot of youth. The shared experiences of the gas shortages of the 1970s, Iran's taking of hostages, and watching the turbulent events of that decade unfold culminated in the election of President Ronald Reagan, a true leader. The subsequent freeing of the American hostages held by Iran for over a year gave us all a sense of American pride and American exceptionalism. Many "Reagan Democrats" were born that day of inauguration, and this is essentially what today's Republican party is all about.

Without the means to afford college, he joined Army ROTC and earned a scholarship to study economics at Fordham University, where he later completed a master's degree. He enrolled in the PhD program, but the world shifted again after 9/11, and he had to put those plans on hold and settle into family life. He has struggled to keep their lives together ever since.

Perseverance and resilience can see you through just about anything, as he would say, and America has always had the ability to reinvent itself if we put freedom, choice and the dignity of the family and individual before all else.

This book is an attempt to capture the essence of that spirit, to shine a light on the struggles and triumphs of everyday Americans who are just trying to make their way in an increasingly complex world while they see their children and families under attack.

To help explain some more of the complex issues in a way that makes sense or common sense for parents through reflection of solid experiences.

Contents

Dedication i
Acknowledgment ii
About The Author iii
Introduction 1
Chapter 1: U.S. – 11.0 Current State Of Affairs And The Destruction Of The Family 8
Chapter 2: Family – A Dying Breed 45
Chapter 3: Public And Private Education And Parental Choice 73
Chapter 4: True Freedom Of The Press: Can It Ever Happen? 99
Chapter 5: Stop The Bleeding: Immigration, Judges, Crime And Honest Elections 113
Chapter 6: Capitalism: Time To Unleash Its True Power 131
Chapter 7: United States 12.0 – Elimination Of C.F.S.M By Empowering Parents And Family 169

Introduction

COVID-19 tyranny changed everything for families in America.

When Donald Trump defeated Hillary Clinton in the 2016 presidential election, it sparked shock and relief. Many conservatives felt relief at avoiding a candidate seen as an extension of the Marxist Obama years.

However, we were naive to think Trump would receive a fair chance to demonstrate his leadership. From day one, he faced attacks from all avenues, and now including assassination attempts. The radical left seemed and still seems intent on undermining him by any means necessary.

Today, we continue to seek answers about numerous critical issues: the origins of COVID, irregularities in the 2020 election, the glaring imbalance in our justice system, the barrage of legal battles against non-communist political leaders, and the ongoing influx of illegal immigrants, often at the expense of American citizens. However, dwelling on past transgressions is only helpful if we use it to develop a path forward, which is what we will try to do.

As parents today, it feels nearly impossible to make sense of it all. Each day, we encounter contradictory opinions from a corporate media complex that excels at manipulating information and the speed at which we see it. What chance do we really have at understanding the truth if we are so barraged with voluminous and conflicting information?

Amid this overwhelming noise and pervasive fear, families are beginning to close ranks if they can or break apart. This is a precursor to the "New Dark Ages." The convergence of today's events is not unique in history. This realization has motivated me to author this book, with the goal of helping families navigate some of the complexities and threats posed by the specter of Communism, as well as other challenges we face today.

I have observed that many Americans are ill-informed and armed with "activist facts" or "one-sided facts." This lack of sensible knowledge extends beyond borders, which has prompted me to explore why there's an imbalance.

Is it ignorance? Is it intellect? Or is it something more sinister? I believe it is the latter. These days, it can be challenging for any individual or family to have access to the complete set of facts needed to thoroughly reason through and arrive at a well-informed position, as was taught to me during my formative years at Fordham with the Jesuits and beyond.

There are so many outlets that call themselves news organizations that blend with amoral social media organizations, which in turn blend with nefarious corporations, which now blend with the tyrannical government... true fascism and to that end, it's impossible to reason out a position, for the average person and so we name the new communist the C.F.S.M communist as all seem bundled or tied together. Middle-class families need more financial power... power, and freedom to raise their

UNITED STATES 12.0 – FREEDOM VS. COMMUNISM

families in the way they want, to choose education, to choose healthcare, to choose true representation and to overcome bureaucrats at all levels. Middle-class families are the truest and strongest opponents of the C.F.S.M communists, and they need help as they are the target.

In Ronald Reagan's inaugural address in 1981, he mentioned a soldier from World War One named Martin Treptow. Martin Treptow was, by all accounts, a true patriot and the truest of all Americans as he left his job to go off and fight in World War 1. As Ronald Reagan relays in his speech, he was killed, and in his possession was a diary, and on the fly leaf, it read:

"America must win this war. Therefore, I will work, I will save, I will sacrifice, I will endure, I will fight cheerfully and do my utmost as if the issue of the whole struggle depended on me alone."

In my view, the U.S. is in the midst of yet another war, but this one is internal, and in order to win, it is up to each and every one of us to embrace the sentiment in the words of Martin Treptow.

This is another "rip apart," this time since 9-11-2001, and now a potential "upgrade" in 2024. By count, we are at version 12.0 in 2024 when compared to the major eras of American history:

- 1492 – Columbus discovery era – American Renaissance and the end of the global Dark Ages

- 1600-1620s – Pilgrimage and Powhatan Indians, and Pocahontas era - Religious Freedom, Indentured Servitude with Family at the core while the Indian wars were just beginning.

- 1776 – Independence/constitution/capitalism era - Revolution to govern ourselves with our God-given rights of liberty and justice. End of British rule.

- 1800s – US expansion era - Manifest Destiny concept essentially revolved around the concept of security of our nation and its families in securing and expanding the U.S.

- 1865 – Civil War/Lincoln era - The defeat of the **democratic** party, the end of slavery, and the beginning of healing with the dignity of the human being at its core.

- 1900 – Industrial Age era - America announces to the world that we are powerful, and our way of life thrives. Massive change, along with massive legal immigration

- 1929 – Excess & Depression era - Reality check to all Americans and learning from our economic and life errors and first implementation of Socialism via Social Security

UNITED STATES 12.0 – FREEDOM VS. COMMUNISM

- 1941- Global War era - The world as we know it almost ended, and true fascism, Marxism and communism would have taken over if we didn't fight with everything we had

- 1965 – "Fake Great Society" era - Lyndon Johnson is the father of democratic socialism, which decimated the black family unit first and spread to all units as we know it

- 1980 – Ronald Regan Freedom era - A true wake-up period to show that government isn't the answer, but it is the problem. Opportunities flourished, as did the family

- 2001 – 9/11 Terrorism era - Darkest day in modern history as religious zealots struck fear into millions, and it opened the door for more government control again and allowed Communism and Marxism to grow and now

- 2024 – End of Covid tyranny, Resurgence of Freedom and The Family era. Defeating communism by empowering our middle class with micro policies aimed at strengthening the Family Unit at all levels

Each time, our nation has found a way to adapt and evolve and become better for it. I have no doubt there will be more transformations to come, but through it all, the core values and pioneering spirit of America must and will endure.

DEFINITIONS FAMILIES NEED TO KNOW:
(Paraphrased from Wikipedia)

Communism – Totalitarian system of government in which a single authoritarian party controls state-owned means of production; the final stage of society in "Marxist" theory in which the state has withered away, and economic goods are distributed equitably. Fascism – Starts out as socialism and ends in autocratic or tyrannical rule; severe collusion between government and big business with social regimentation and forcible suppression of opposition in many ways, including censorship.

Marxism – Advocated by Karl Marx - A theory of practice of "socialism," class struggle, Capitalist exploitation of labor, dialectical materialism and the dictatorship of the proletariat leading to a classless society and Communism.

Socialism – Collective or Governmental ownership and administration of the means of production and distribution of goods and services; no private property; A stage of society in "Marxist" theory that is transitional between "Capitalism" and "Communism" or "Fascism."

Capitalism – an economic system based on freedom and choice whereby the private or corporate ownership of capital goods and private property is obtained through investments that are determined by free private decision makers. Determined by prices, production, and the distribution of goods through fair competition in a free market. Throughout this book, the terms communism, socialism, fascism, and

Marxism will be interchanged and, from a family perspective, are synonymous and ought to be viewed as one evil term, "C.F.S.M COMMUNIST," as each is being applied in various degrees in different areas with distinctions often quite difficult to pinpoint. However, the overall goal is the same: elimination of the middle class and dominance of us all.

The trends in this country are clearly leaning towards "C.F.S.M communist," and it is important to note that in order for "C.F.S.M communist" to succeed, the independent middle-class family unit must cease to exist, and the question that you need to ask yourself is how do they accomplish that?

Answer: They must eliminate the family connections, erode financial security, degrade morality and reduce in class the entire middle-class family unit as we know it.

Tyrannical people naturally gravitate to "C.F.S.M communism" as it consolidates their power, but they also need money to function, and so, therefore, they must be very closely aligned with big business. Big businesses also need to be closely aligned with them as they are just as integral. Both rule over the lowest class of society, which is also the neediest class of society. What true C.F.S.M communists do not need are independent, financially solvent, free-thinking families. They are an obstacle to everything the C.F.S.M communists are trying to achieve…centralized control and complete domination.

We must all play a part to stop them.

Chapter 1: U.S. – 11.0 Current State of Affairs and the Destruction of the Family

As we stand at this crucial juncture in American history, it is impossible to ignore the tumultuous winds of change sweeping across our great nation. The United States of America, long heralded as a bastion of freedom, democracy, and opportunity, finds itself once again at a crossroads for the 12th time. We are in the midst of another attempt to fundamentally alter the fabric of our society, to reshape the very foundations upon which this country was built. This change, if left unchecked, threatens to erode the values and principles that have made America the envy of the world for generations.

The gravity of our current situation cannot be overstated. We are witnessing a concerted effort to redefine what it means to be American, to question the validity of our institutions, and to undermine the pillars of our democratic republic. This is not merely a difference of political opinion or a natural evolution of societal norms. Rather, it is a calculated attempt to dismantle the America we know and love, replacing it with a vision that is fundamentally at odds with the ideals of our Founding Fathers.

When you see the attention that C.F.S.M communist books like Howard Zinn's "People's History of the United States" get from Gen Z, even though it is replete with all types of false information, you can then get a sense of how deep the C.F.S.M communist sentiment goes. Mary Grabar's books, especially "Debunking Howard Zinn: Exposing the Fake History That Turned a Generation Against America," especially regarding the denigration and maligning of Christopher Columbus' and his discovery of America, is TRULY a MUST read by anyone in the academic field seeking truth.

As concerned citizens, it is our solemn duty to recognize the dangers that lie ahead and to take decisive action to preserve our nation. We must stand united against those who seek to divide us, sow discord among our communities, and weaken the bonds that have held our diverse nation together for centuries. The task before us is not an easy one, but it is one that we must undertake with unwavering resolve and determination.

In the pages that follow, we will explore the various facets of this attempted transformation, examining the forces at work and the potential consequences of their success. We will delve into the historical parallels that can inform our understanding of the present, and we will outline the steps we must take to safeguard our republic for future generations.

The time for complacency has long since passed. We can no longer afford to be passive observers as our nation is reshaped before our very eyes, and not for the better. It is incumbent upon every one of us to become active participants in the preservation of our American way of life.

We must educate ourselves, engage in meaningful dialogue with our fellow citizens, and take concrete actions both locally and nationally to protect the freedoms and opportunities that have defined our nation since its inception.

As we embark on this journey together, let us remember the words of Thomas Jefferson: "The price of freedom is eternal vigilance." Now, more than ever, we must remain vigilant in the face of those who would seek to fundamentally alter the course of our nation. We must stand firm in our commitment to the principles of liberty, justice, and equality that have guided us through our darkest hours and our greatest triumphs.

On the cover of this book is the traditional nuclear American family, and it is in the middle of all the tumultuous historical events as the family unit is the center of our collective moral universe.

The chapters that follow will serve as a call to action, a rallying cry for all those who believe in the promise of America. Together, we can stem the tide of destructive change and ensure that the United States remains a shining city upon a hill, a beacon of hope and freedom for the world.

America and Ancient Rome

To truly understand the gravity of our current situation, we must look to the annals of history for guidance and perspective. The rise and fall of great civilizations throughout the ages can provide valuable insights into the challenges we face today. Perhaps no historical parallel is more apt or more sobering than that of Ancient Rome, whose decline and ultimate fall bear striking similarities to the predicament in which America now finds itself.

Rome, once the undisputed superpower of the ancient world, stood as a testament to human achievement, innovation, and governance. For centuries, the Roman Empire was the epitome of civilization, boasting advanced infrastructure, a sophisticated legal system, and unparalleled military might. Yet, despite its seemingly unassailable position, Rome fell to invading forces in 410 AD, marking the end of an era and the beginning of the "Dark Ages," which lasted over 1,000 years.

The human suffering that followed the fall of Rome was nothing short of epic and is something every family should strive to understand and avoid.

The factors that contributed to Rome's downfall were numerous and complex, but three key issues stand out as particularly relevant to our current American experience: fiscal instability, lawfare, and political corruption.

Fiscal Instability:

In its later years, the Roman Empire faced severe economic challenges. The cost of maintaining a vast empire, coupled with declining productivity and a debased currency, led to crippling inflation and economic stagnation. The government resorted to excessive taxation and currency devaluation to fund its military and operations, placing an enormous burden on the populace and eroding the foundations of Roman prosperity and security.

Today, we see alarming parallels in the United States. Our national debt has reached unprecedented levels (35 Trillion with another 7 Trillion on the Fed's balance sheet = 42+ Trillion), with government spending far outpacing tax revenue. The Federal Reserve's globally focused monetary policies, coupled with irresponsible government spending, have led to concerns about inflation and the devaluation of the dollar. Just as in Rome, these fiscal challenges threaten to undermine the economic stability that has been a cornerstone of American strength.

Lawfare:

The Roman legal system, once a model of justice and order, became increasingly weaponized, especially prior to the Julius Caesar period and in the ending years of the empire. Political opponents used the courts to attack and undermine each other, eroding public trust in the institutions meant to uphold the rule of law.

The legal process became a tool for settling personal vendettas rather than a means of ensuring justice and societal order. Prior to Julius Caesar, lawfare led directly to tyranny through Emperors, and at the end of the empire, it led to its destruction. Lawfare is a short-term means to an end to gain power In modern America, we are witnessing a similar phenomenon. The justice system is increasingly being used as a political weapon, with investigations and prosecutions motivated more by partisan interests than by a genuine pursuit of justice. This erosion of faith in our legal institutions threatens the very fabric of our constitutional republic in our democratic society.

Political Corruption:

As Rome's power grew, so too did the opportunities for corruption among its ruling class. Senators and officials often prioritized their personal interests over those of the state, leading to a breakdown in effective governance.

The Roman people became increasingly disillusioned with their leaders, eroding the social contract that had held the empire together for centuries. In a truly tyrannical fashion, Rome evolved into 2 classes: the poor and the rich. As the middle class was eliminated, so was the family unit, which was the core that Rome could no longer pilfer from for its wars.

The United States today faces its own crisis of political corruption. The influence of special interest groups, the revolving door between government and private industry, and the perception that politicians are more concerned with re-election and enriching themselves than with serving their constituents have all contributed to a growing sense of distrust in our political system. The parallels between the fall of Rome and the current situation in America are both striking and deeply concerning. Just as Rome's decline was not the result of a single catastrophic event but rather a **gradual erosion** of its foundational strengths, so too do we face a multifaceted threat to the pillars of our republic.

However, it is crucial to note that while these parallels are instructive, they are not deterministic. The United States, unlike Rome, has the benefit of historical hindsight and the tools of modern democracy at its disposal. We have the opportunity to learn from Rome's mistakes and take corrective action before it is too late. Will we?

As we examine the challenges facing our nation, we must keep in mind the lessons of Rome's fall. We must address our fiscal instability, protect the integrity of our legal system, and root out corruption at all levels of government. Only by confronting these issues head-on can we hope to avoid the fate that befell one of history's greatest civilizations.

The fall of Rome serves as a stark reminder of the fragility of even the mightiest empires. It is a call to action for all Americans who value the principles upon which our nation was founded.

We must remain vigilant, engaged, and committed to preserving the United States as a beacon of freedom and constitutional republic for generations to come, and it all begins and ends with strengthening the family unit and middle class.

The State of Disunion

As we turn our attention to the present state of our nation, it becomes painfully clear that the United States is experiencing a level of division and discord not seen since the tumultuous days of the Civil War and the 1960's. The fabric of our society, once woven tightly with threads of shared values and common purpose, now appears frayed and tattered. This state of disunion threatens not only our ability to govern effectively but also the very essence of what it means to be American.

At the heart of this division lies a profound breakdown in communication and understanding between different segments of our population. We have become a nation of echo chambers, where individuals increasingly surround themselves only with those who share their views, leading to a dangerous polarization of thought and ideology. This polarization has been exacerbated by the rise of social media and the 24-hour news cycle, which often prioritizes sensationalism and conflict over nuanced discussion and mutual understanding.

One of the most glaring examples of this growing division can be seen in the realm of race relations. It is with great sadness and concern that we must acknowledge the role that former President Barack Obama played in this deterioration.

Despite the historic nature of his presidency and the hope it initially inspired, Obama's tenure ultimately set race relations back by decades, stoking hatred and victimization instead of building the bridges of understanding and reconciliation that our nation so desperately needed after the attack and post 9-11-2001. Obama's approach to racial issues often seemed to emphasize differences rather than commonalities, highlighting grievances instead of promoting unity. His rhetoric, while perhaps eloquent, frequently served to deepen existing racial divides rather than heal them. By focusing on historical injustices without adequately acknowledging the progress made, Obama's administration contributed to a climate of resentment and mistrust between different racial communities and classes.

This is not to say that racial inequality and injustice do not exist in America. They do, and they must always be addressed. However, the approach taken during the Obama years often seemed to pit different racial and class groups against each other rather than fostering a sense of shared American identity that transcends racial and class boundaries.

The consequences of this divisive approach have been far-reaching and deeply damaging to the social fabric of our nation. We have witnessed an alarming increase in racial tensions, with incidents of racial violence and unrest becoming all too common as all events are amplified.

The rise of identity politics has further fragmented our society, encouraging individuals to view themselves primarily through the lens of race, gender, or other demographic categories rather than as Americans united by common values and aspirations. This state of disunion extends far beyond racial issues. We see it in the growing urban-rural divide, where citizens in different parts of the country seem to inhabit entirely different realities. We see it in the widening gap between the wealthy and the working class, fueling resentment and social unrest. The term "pay your fair share" is the C.F.S.M activist's favorite tool. We see it in the bitter partisanship that has paralyzed our political system, making it nearly impossible to address the pressing challenges facing our nation.

The consequences of this disunion are severe and far-reaching. It has eroded trust in our institutions, from government to media to education. It has made it increasingly difficult to find common ground on even the most basic issues facing our society.

Most alarmingly, it has opened the door for extremist ideologies to gain a foothold as people search for simple answers to complex problems, especially amongst the younger, more impressionable; communism has come back out of the darkness and is now in the light.

This state of disunion is not merely a matter of differing opinions or healthy debate. It represents a fundamental threat to the stability and future of our republic. A house divided against itself cannot stand, as Abraham Lincoln famously warned. If we cannot find a way to bridge these divides and rediscover our shared American identity, we risk losing the very essence of what has made our nation great, and we should NEVER be ashamed of the greatness that is America. The path forward will not be easy, but it is one we must traverse together. We must reject the politics of division and embrace a vision of America that is unifying and grounded in our shared values of freedom, opportunity, and justice for all. We must learn to listen to one another, to seek understanding rather than confrontation, and to find common ground even in the face of disagreement.

This does not mean abandoning our principles or ignoring real issues of injustice. Rather, it means approaching these challenges with a spirit of good faith and a commitment to finding solutions that benefit all Americans. It means recognizing that our diversity is a strength, not a weakness when it is united by a shared commitment to the American dream.

As we move forward, we must also be vigilant against those who would seek to exploit our divisions for their own gain. Whether they are foreign adversaries seeking to sow discord or domestic actors pursuing narrow ideological agendas, we must stand united against attempts to further fragment our society.

The state of disunion in which we find ourselves is a crisis, but it is also an opportunity. It is a chance for us to reaffirm our commitment to the ideals that have always defined America at its best. It is a moment for us to recommit ourselves to the arduous work of democracy, to engage in difficult conversations and make the tough compromises necessary to move our nation forward. As we confront this challenge, let us draw inspiration from the words of Martin Luther King Jr., who reminded us that "we may have all come on different ships, but we're in the same boat now." Our fate as a nation is inextricably linked, and only by coming together can we hope to navigate the turbulent waters ahead.

The state of disunion we face is real and pressing, but it is not insurmountable. With courage, compassion, and a renewed commitment to our shared American Family values, we can bridge the divides that separate us and emerge stronger and more united than ever before. This is the challenge of our time, and it is one that we must meet with unwavering resolve and determination.

The Influence of Modern Communism

As we delve deeper into the challenges facing our nation, we must confront an uncomfortable truth: many of the issues plaguing America today can be traced back to the insidious influence of communist ideology. While the Cold War may have ended decades ago, the specter of communism and tyranny reminiscent of the past and akin to the "Dark Ages," continues to haunt our way of life, manifesting itself in various forms that threaten the very foundations of our democratic republic.

It is crucial to understand that modern communism is not always overtly labeled as such. Instead, it often hides behind more palatable terms like "progressivism," "DEI," or "social justice." However, at its core, it still seeks to fundamentally transform our society, eroding individual liberties by pitting one group against another and concentrating power in the hands of an elite few. Let us examine how this communist influence has seeped into various aspects of American life:

1. Crime and the Push to Federalize Law Enforcement:

It is crucial to understand that communism thrives in chaos, turmoil, and oppression at the middle-class level. Freedom is antithetical to its principles and must be suppressed at all costs.

One method the C.F.S.M communists utilize to create chaos and instability is by funding radical prosecutors and attorneys general, who then take positions of power in major cities.

These C.F.S.M officials allow dangerous criminals back onto the streets and contribute to the destabilization of the state. There are too many of these individuals out there, and they all must be stopped.

This is part of the most alarming of trends. We are witnessing the deliberate undermining of law and order in our communities. The push to "defund the police" and the demonization of law enforcement officers, in general, are not merely misguided policy proposals; they are part of a calculated effort to create chaos and instability so that people will be forced to turn to the GOVERNMENT for solutions.

As Ronald Reagan so eloquently put it, "**The nine most terrifying words in the English language are: I'm from the Government, and I'm here to help.**"

By weakening local law enforcement, the C.F.S.M movement aims to create a power vacuum that can only be filled by a centralized federal police force. This goes a long way toward explaining the seeming collusion between the ATF, FBI, DOJ, IRS, CIA, DOS and HLS.

How else can you get 51 former "intelligence" officials to all lie so quickly about fake "Russian interference" – all to stop Donald Trump from being elected? It is Collusion mixed with C.F.S.M in order to keep the C.F.S.M machine moving forward; none of them want to lose their "party status."

Taking out local law enforcement would be a significant step towards the type of authoritarian control that is a hallmark of communist regimes. We must resist these efforts and support our local law enforcement agencies, ensuring they have the resources and support needed to keep our communities safe.

2.Immigration, Invasion and the Goal of Destabilization:

Another aspect of the C.F.S.M communist agenda is mass immigration, which has caused immense destabilization in our society. Weak borders are a threat to our nation's survival and every other civilization before us. The true motives behind this influx of immigrants are sinister and have nothing to do with humanitarian aid or progress. If they did, immediate action would be taken to stop the rampant cartel activity, sex trafficking, and human slavery that result from this uncontrolled flow of people. The ongoing crisis at our southern border is not merely a result of poor policy decisions; it is a deliberate attempt to destabilize our nation through sheer volume. By encouraging and facilitating mass illegal immigration, communist-inspired forces seek to overwhelm our generous social systems, dilute our national identity, water down American citizenship, and, most importantly, create a dependent class that can be easily manipulated for political gain.

If you have any doubt about this tactic, just look at what the "Great Society" programs did to the black family unit primarily and how dependent that one group became on the government for survival.

This culminated in over 90% support for Democratic party voting for decades. If the model didn't work, they wouldn't use it, except this time, they are going too far, too fast, and it has and will backfire.

This is not to say that all immigrants are part of this scheme. Many come to America legally seeking a better life and embrace our values wholeheartedly. We all welcome legal immigrants, as all our families descended from immigrants at one point or another. However, the current situation, with its open borders and lax enforcement of immigration laws, is clearly designed to serve a larger, more nefarious purpose.

UNITED STATES 12.0 – FREEDOM VS. COMMUNISM

3. Censorship as a Tool of Control:

One of the most fundamental principles of a free society is the right to free speech. Yet, we are witnessing an unprecedented assault on this right, with big tech companies, mainstream media, and even government agencies colluding to silence dissenting voices. COVID speech control under the Biden administration retaught us all how true fascism works between government and big business. The coercive collusion between social media companies and the government to control speech is fascism at its best. This fascism cost lives during COVID, a lot of which were lost due to the suppression of treatments that worked in other parts of the world, all to set the stage to control speech in the election process under the guise of "misinformation."

This censorship is straight out of the communist C.F.S.M playbook. By controlling the flow of information, they seek to shape public opinion and stifle any opposition to their agenda. We must fight against this censorship with all our might, defending the right of all Americans to speak freely and access diverse viewpoints regardless of whether they hurt the feelings of individuals or groups.

The goal of the C.F.S.M communists is to infiltrate and attack the United States from within. Their actions must be met with strong opposition before it's too late. Communism just doesn't happen overnight. Khrushchev, the Russian leader who was a staunch communist, continually opposed capitalism. Many false claims were attributed to him for stating that The US would be fed socialism in small doses until one day it became communism. However, whether he said that during speeches is debatable, but the sentiment behind it rings true, and ultimately, that's what's happened.

Make no mistake, the seeds of socialism that the Cold War left in its wake are bearing crops in true communism today.

4. Bureaucratic Power Vacuums:

The growth of the administrative state is perhaps one of the most insidious ways in which communist ideology has infiltrated our government. Unelected bureaucrats in agencies like the FBI, DOJ, DOE, DOD, ATF, EPA, CIA, and IRS, courtesy of the Obama transformation, wield enormous power, often with little accountability to the American people.

These agencies, originally created to serve specific functions, have become bloated power centers that often work against the interests of the very citizens they are meant to serve. The C.F.S.M communist influence is evident in their tendency to expand their authority, regulate every aspect of our lives, and prioritize their own power over the well-being of the nation.

Over the years, we have come to respect these agencies as they have always had our best interests at heart; however, in recent years, these agencies have become weaponized and have lost the trust of the American people. As a matter of fact, bringing in 20 million new people every year devoids any trust that was even there since you are metamorphizing the country into "useful idiots," as Lenin would say. In another example, the Department of Justice (DOJ) recently put out 12 specific crimes to use against parents for parents who are addressing educational community boards contentiously and conscientiously. It is precisely activities and actions like this that undermine the trust that families have in our own government now.

5. Education as Indoctrination:

Our education system, from elementary schools to universities, has become a breeding ground for communist C.F.S.M ideas. Under the guise of "critical thinking" and "social justice," many educators are indoctrinating our youth with ideologies that are fundamentally at odds with American values and, more importantly, their own families.

This isn't education; it's propaganda to convert a generation or two. By both rewriting and using revisionist history, promoting divisive concepts like Critical Race Theory (CRT), and demonizing individualism, self-reliance and capitalism, these educators are shaping a generation that is increasingly hostile to the very principles upon which our nation and family base was founded.

This is extremely reminiscent of Hitler's youth movement, where the intent was to pit the youth against their parents to engender loyalty to the state, and it worked. There isn't a parent today who doesn't have a child or two who are strongly resisting societal norms and pushing back against their own families, and the pain is real. As a response, many parents try to take on a more friendly, approachable role in the hopes of preserving the family unit. However, the challenges facing modern families are often too powerful for parents to overcome on their own.

6. The Role of Non-Governmental Organizations (NGOs):

There are over 1.5 million NGOs registered in our country. Many NGOs, while claiming to work for social good, are, in fact, vehicles for spreading communist C.F.S.M ideology, and they are impossible to root out. These organizations, often funded by wealthy donors with questionable motives, work to undermine our institutions, promote divisive ideologies, and advance policies that weaken our nation. Can you imagine that George Soros and Bill Gates probably get tax breaks for funding many of these NGOs?

We must be vigilant in scrutinizing these organizations and their true objectives. Many of them operate under the guise of philanthropy but are actually working to reshape our society in ways that are antithetical to American values.

This is one of the biggest loopholes in our tax code and is fundamentally juxtaposed with our constitution, given the ideologies that are fomented by these NGOs. And they must be stopped, and the only way to do this is through the IRS. It should be done in the same way Lois Lerner took out the Tea Party nonprofits by restricting and delaying tax status, amongst other things, as they made steady progress against the Obama administration. Nothing has ever happened to her, but the damage is done, and we must do the same to root this evil out.

The Threat to Family's Freedom:

It is crucial to understand that communism thrives when and as freedom dies. The two ideologies cannot coexist with each other. The end goal of all these efforts is to create a society where individual liberty is subordinated to the will of the state. By eroding our freedoms **bit by bit**, under the guise of safety, equality, or social justice, communist-inspired forces seek to fundamentally transform America into something unrecognizable to those who cherish liberty. The changes are designed to be minute, all of it beginning slowly with the intent of being utilized at a later point in time.

Today, you are restricted from voicing an opinion on values at a school board or even at your place of employment. Tomorrow, you will be arrested for it.

The power of unelected bureaucrats, the erosion of local authority, the assault on free speech, the indoctrination of our youth, and the importance of over 20m illegal immigrants are all part of a larger strategy to centralize power and control every aspect of our lives. This is the very antithesis of the American dream for all American families. Ironically, it will also be a surprise to the illegal immigrant families who are coming here for what we were, not what we are becoming. The principles upon which our nation was founded will all be changed, and we will enter a new "Dark Age."

Checks and Balances:

One of the cornerstone principles of the American constitutional republic is the system of checks and balances designed by our Founding Fathers - some of the most brilliant political thinkers of their era. This system was intentionally designed to prevent any single branch of government from accumulating too much power while also restricting the government's reach.

However, the communist influence we're witnessing today seeks to undermine this and many crucial safeguards.

By expanding the power of the executive branch through executive orders and regulatory agencies, by packing and expanding the courts with ideologically aligned judges, and by weakening the legislative branch through gridlock and partisanship, communist-inspired forces are slowly eroding the checks and balances that have protected our democratic republic for centuries. The **last and ultimate** check pertains to fair and honest elections because the citizen is the ultimate check on all three branches of government, and now the election process is under attack by our own government as well. No, this is not Donald Trump, who has continually been demonized as an enemy of democracy. Quite frankly, the statement is pure projection and is the greatest farce ever created. This movement was created by the radical left, and today's radical Democrat is a C.F.S.M, which is where you will find the origins of this movement. We must fight to restore these checks and balances, ensuring that power remains distributed and that no single entity – whether it's a government agency, a political party, or a group of unelected bureaucrats – can exert undue influence over our nation's direction ever again, this is a test for us all.

Every government official must be subject to rigorous checks and balances - just as our system of democracy intended. When individuals are given unchecked power, they inevitably abuse it and crave more. Therefore, measures must be put in place to hold these bureaucrats accountable. To start, we must link their salaries to those in the private sector, as an inflated government salary only leads to fiscal disaster.

If executive public sector salaries continue to exceed private sector salaries, we are setting ourselves up for financial failure. By implementing a **freeze** on wage growth and conducting a thorough cleaning of the house, we can begin to rein in these unelected bureaucrats who seek to use their power for nefarious purposes. We must not allow them to perpetuate their control over us any longer.

The Economic Threat:

While traditional communism C.F.S.M focused primarily on state ownership of the means of production, modern communist influence in America takes a more subtle approach. It seeks to undermine our capitalist system through excessive regulation, punitive taxation, destabilization of the criminal justice system, and the promotion of dependency on government programs, as explained earlier. The push for expansive welfare programs, universal basic income, massive child tax credits, and "free" government services is not motivated by compassion but by a desire to create a populace that is reliant on the state. This dependency is a key tool of control, as it makes citizens less likely to challenge the government's authority or question its policies and look the other way.

Furthermore, the demonization of successful businesses and entrepreneurs serves to discourage innovation and economic growth. By painting wealth as inherently evil, communist-inspired ideologues seek to stifle the very engine of prosperity that has made America the most successful nation in history. It makes no sense to be jealous of wealth creators who give people very good start opportunities in life. It is OK to demonize wealth creators who turned political and tried to consolidate their positions of power.

It is as if the world has forgotten the spectacular collapse of the U.S.S.R's communist system in the early 90's through Ronald Reagan's leadership. Everything we are examining leads to this repeat; however, it is important to note that it took millions of lives, countless liberties and many decades of human suffering before the inevitable collapse. The average family doesn't have the tools to understand how they are being attacked as this is analogous to the storied frog that is slowly boiled to death by increasing the temperature only 1 degree at a time…until death.

Cultural Marxism:

Another critical aspect of communist influence in America is the concept and intertwining of Cultural Marxism. This ideology seeks to apply Marxist **class struggle** theory to cultural issues, pitting different groups against each other based on race, gender, sexual orientation, and other identities. Things and groups like BLM (Black Lives Matter), ANTIFA, CRT, DEI, White Supremacy, Alpha Male Aggression, Gender issues for kids, Catholics and Latin Mass (hard to believe that one) are all designed to create victims and destroy the family as they are all designed to pit one group against another to create chaos.

The result is a fragmented society where individuals are encouraged to see themselves primarily as members of oppressed or oppressor groups rather than as unified Americans. This divisive ideology undermines social cohesion and national unity, making it easier for communist-inspired C.F.S.M forces to exert control over a divided populace.

We see the effects of Cultural Marxism in the rise of identity politics, the promotion of victimhood culture, and the increasing hostility towards traditional American values and institutions. Whether the term is cultural Marxism, fascism, communism, democratic socialism, or just straight socialism, they all have blurred lines to start, but the intent at the finish line is all the same… human control, the birth of C.F.S.M is here.

The Role of Media:

The mainstream media, once a watchdog of free speech, has, in many cases, become a mouthpiece for communist-inspired ideologies, and it's all for money. Through selective reporting, biased analysis, and outright propaganda, many media outlets are shaping public opinion in ways that align with a communist worldview.

This manipulation of information is a powerful tool for control. By controlling the narrative, these media entities can influence elections, shape policy debates, and even rewrite history to suit their agenda.

We must encourage critical thinking and media literacy among all Americans, empowering them to seek out diverse sources of information and come to their own conclusions rather than blindly accepting the narratives pushed by biased media outlets.

However, this cannot happen while media companies are predominantly owned by corporate entities. For these corporations, media outlets often serve merely as vocal public relations tools. This creates a clear conflict of interest, as the media becomes dependent on the corporation for financial existence.

The Threat to National Sovereignty:

Communist or C.F.S.M influence also manifests in efforts to undermine national sovereignty. This can be seen in the push for globalist policies that prioritize international agreements over American interests, such as the "Paris Climate Accords," the promotion of open borders, and the denigration of patriotism and citizenship as a form of bigotry or even imperialism. The process for treaties has devolved into Presidential executive orders, which are highly political. This is NOT how the process is supposed to work. The Senate is supposed to ratify all negotiated treaties by a 2/3 majority.

This means that 67 Senators must all agree, and that is what commits the U.S., NOT presidential executive orders. The "Paris Accords" are NOT ratified and should NOT bind America until the Senate agrees to ratify.

By weakening our national identity and our borders, these forces seek to create a world where nation-states are less relevant, paving the way for a system of global governance that aligns closely with communist ideals, and every day, we are inching one step closer. America itself IS the problem and the biggest obstacle to this new world order.

It is extremely important to note that national sovereignty can never be dissipated in a country where the family unit is strong. Therefore, the number one tool of the communist C.F.S.M must be the destruction of the family unit, and to do that, they must destroy everything that is important to a family, such as moral values, religion, culture and identity. This all starts by usurping the authority of the parent, then the family. It's exactly why we need to fix this problem at its core.

The Way Forward:

Recognizing the pervasive influence of communist C.F.S.M ideology in our society is the first step towards combating it. We must be vigilant in identifying these threats and steadfast in our defense of American values and institutions.

This means Empowering Parents First:

1. Empowering Parents by Promoting education choices that teach true American history and civics, instilling a sense of pride in our nation's accomplishments while honestly addressing its shortcomings.

2. Empowering Parents by Supporting financial taxation policies that protect children and encourage individual responsibility, free enterprise, and limited government.

3. Empowering Parents to Defend free speech and push back against censorship and tyranny in all its forms without the FBI targeting them.

4. Empowering Parents to help protect their families and their children by protecting the rights of the 2nd Amendment and enforcing our immigration laws to maintain national sovereignty.

5. Empowering Parents to help Reform our bureaucratic agencies through honest, transparent and fair elections to ensure they serve the American people rather than their own interests.

6. Empower Parents to Encourage critical thinking with their children and support diverse viewpoints in our educational institutions and media landscape according to their shared American assimilated moral values.

7. Empower Parents to reject divisive ideologies in schools that seek to fragment our society and instead promote a unifying vision of American identity without reprisal from the FBI.

The battle against communist C.F.S.M influence in America is not just about politics or economics; it's about preserving the very soul of our nation. It's about ensuring that future generations inherit a country that is free, prosperous, and true to the principles upon which it was founded. A free and morally protected child leads to true defenders of liberty.

As we face this challenge, let us draw inspiration from the words of Ronald Reagan: **"Freedom is never more than one generation away from extinction. We didn't pass it to our children in the bloodstream. It must be fought for, protected, and handed on for them to do the same."**

The fight against communist C.F.S.M influence in America is the fight for freedom itself. It is a fight we must engage in with unwavering resolve, for the stakes cannot be higher. Our actions today will determine whether America remains a beacon of liberty for the world or succumbs to the destructive ideologies that have brought ruin to so many nations throughout history.

Shrinking the Size and Power of Government

As we confront the challenges posed by communist C.F.S.M influence and the erosion of our freedoms, one of the most crucial steps we must take is to significantly reduce the size and power of our government. The bloated federal bureaucracy that has grown over decades not only stifles individual liberty and economic prosperity but also provides fertile ground for the spread of communist-inspired C.F.S.M ideologies within our institutions.

The Founders' Vision:

When our Founding Fathers crafted the Constitution, they envisioned a **limited** federal government with enumerated powers, leaving the bulk of governance to the states and the people.

This design was intentional and aimed at preventing the concentration of power that could lead to tyranny, as history taught them all. At the time, we didn't even have a central bank for the same control reason, but now we have central banks that even coordinate their efforts in a global cabal. The concept of "too big to fail" will ruin America as the collusion between government and big business will never end and increase fascist rule, if we don't allow corporations to fail and new, healthier ones to grow. However, over the years, particularly since the "New Deal" era and further cemented in place with the "Great Society" era, we have witnessed a steady **expansion** of federal power far beyond what the Founders intended. This growth has come at the expense of state authority, individual liberty, family and economic freedom. I believe it has reached its tipping point, and it needs to head back down. It all begins with the family.

While it's true that the COVID government crackdown on free speech was a severe limitation to our rights, it is not the first time that the government has stepped in and usurped the individual liberties we so much enjoyed.

The genesis of the financial collapse of 2008 began in the late 90s, driven by overly liberalized housing policies under then Housing Secretary Andrew Cuomo and Clinton that forced banks to lend generously to unqualified borrowers. This was further exacerbated by risky financial instruments like derivatives that tied multiple financially bad homes to a few good homes, leading to a cascade of economic devastation. In response, the government stepped in to address the fallout from these poor liberal policies combined with greed and collusion.

The Dangers of Big Government Are Clear:

1. **Erosion of Individual Liberty:** As the government grows, it inevitably encroaches on areas of life that should be left to individual choice. From healthcare decisions to educational choices, big government seeks to dictate how we live our lives, undermining personal responsibility and freedom.

2. **Economic Stagnation:** Excessive regulation and high taxation are hallmarks of big government and

stifle innovation and economic growth. They create barriers to entry for new businesses and impose burdensome compliance costs on existing ones, leading to reduced productivity and job creation.

3. **Inefficiency and Waste:** Large bureaucracies are inherently inefficient. They are slow to adapt, prone to waste, and often prioritize self-preservation over serving the public interest.

4. **Corruption and Cronyism:** The bigger the government, the more opportunities there are for corruption. Special interests and lobbyists wield undue influence, leading to policies that benefit the few at the expense of the many.

5. **Dependency:** Expansive government programs create a culture of dependency, discouraging self-reliance and personal responsibility. This dependency makes people more susceptible to government control and manipulation.

6. HUMAN SUFFERING…what more needs to be said?

Steps to Shrink Government:

1. Regulatory Reform: We must undertake a comprehensive review of federal regulations, eliminating those that are unnecessary, outdated, or overly burdensome. This will free businesses to innovate and grow, creating jobs and prosperity and reducing the need for so many bureaucrats.

2. Spending Cuts: Federal spending has reached unsustainable levels. We need to make hard choices, cutting wasteful programs and reducing the size of many federal agencies. This will not only reduce the deficit but also limit the government's ability to interfere in our lives. Spending needs to be tied to congressional salaries along with growth, unemployment and a few other measurement tools.

3. Tax Reform: Simplifying the tax code and reducing tax rates will stimulate economic growth and limit the government's ability to use the tax system as a tool for social engineering to dramatically support the family unit.

4. Decentralization: Many functions currently performed by the federal government should be returned to the states or to the private sector. This aligns with the principle of limited federalism and allows for more localized, responsive governance. At the top of this list is the reduction of federal agencies and moving those dollars into the states so that the states can better utilize their local populace.

5. Term Qualifications, not Term Limits: Implementing term qualifications as a function of private sector experience for members of Congress would help break the cycle of career politicians and bring fresh, grounded perspectives to government. All should have a minimum of **10 years of private sector** experience before entering any office. The goal of a young person should not be to try to control or rule over others. The goal of a young person should be to create something in this capitalist economy and then find a way to give back after they've achieved some experience in the capitalist economy. This alone will solve ALL problems.

6. Civil Service Reform: We need to make it easier to remove ineffective or corrupt government employees, ensuring that our bureaucracies are staffed by individuals committed to serving the public rather than advancing a political agenda. Civil service is a noble service, but we cannot bloat the agencies with ineffective administrative people. We need police, we need trash collectors, we need all types of civil servants, but we don't need bureaucrats and administrators in abundance. The salaries of bureaucrats and administrators **should be less** than those of civil servants, as the goal should be on the task and not on the control of individuals.

7. Education Reform: We must promote school choice and local parental control of education, breaking the monopoly of government-run schools that often serve as incubators for leftist ideologies. Much more to come on this particular topic, but suffice it to say this is the core of parental power that is needed. Parents must take back education. The concept of tenure must be abolished. There should never be a bureaucrat or administrator who doesn't teach ever again. The day of the school administrator is over.

8. Privatization: Many services currently provided by the government could be more efficiently delivered by the private sector. We should explore opportunities for privatization where appropriate.

The Benefits of Smaller Federal Government:

Reducing the size and power of government will yield numerous benefits:

1. **Increased Economic Growth:** With fewer regulations and lower taxes, businesses will be free to innovate and expand, creating jobs and prosperity.

2. **Greater Individual Freedom:** As the government's reach is limited, individuals will have more control over their own lives and decisions.

3. **Improved Efficiency**: Smaller, more focused government agencies can be more responsive and efficient in performing their core functions.

4. **Reduced Corruption:** With fewer opportunities for cronyism and less money flowing through government coffers, corruption will naturally decrease.

5. **Strengthening of States by using the 10th amendment:** Returning "reserved powers" to the states. This will allow for policy experimentation and solutions tailored to local needs.

6. **Fiscal Responsibility:** Reduced spending will help address our national debt and ensure a more stable economic future for coming generations. It is literally impossible for any federal elected official to reduce

spending. **The only way you will ever get spending reductions is by revising the salaries of all government officials to be tied to efficiency, growth and low unemployment. It would literally solve the spending problem overnight.**

Addressing Concerns:

Critics may argue that a shrinking government will lead to the neglect of important social needs. However, history has shown that private charities, community organizations, and local governments are often more effective at addressing social issues than large, impersonal federal bureaucracies.

Moreover, a thriving economy resulting from limited government will generate more resources for addressing societal needs, both through private means and more efficient public programs.

The Path Forward:

Shrinking the size and power of government is not a task that can be accomplished overnight. It will require sustained effort, political will, and the active engagement of citizens who understand the importance of limited government, and it all begins with the family unit.

We must elect leaders who are committed to this vision of smaller government and hold them accountable for following through on their promises. We must also work to educate our fellow citizens about the benefits of limited

UNITED STATES 12.0 – FREEDOM VS. COMMUNISM

government and the dangers of the communist-inspired ideologies that seek to expand state power. As we undertake this crucial task of reducing government, we must remain vigilant against those who would seek to exploit the resulting vacuum for nefarious purposes. The goal is not to create chaos or anarchy but to restore the proper balance between government authority and individual liberty as envisioned by our Founders.

The task of shrinking government and combating communist C.F.S.M influence in our society is daunting, but it is also essential for the preservation of our republic. As Ronald Reagan wisely noted, **"Man is not free unless government is limited."**

By reducing the size and power of government, we can create a more prosperous, free, and truly democratic society. We can unleash the incredible potential of the American people by growing our families and fostering innovation, creativity, and personal responsibility. This is not just about policy changes; it's about reclaiming the American spirit of self-reliance, individual liberty, and limited government that has made our nation great. It's about ensuring that future generations inherit a country where opportunity is abundant, liberty is cherished, and the pursuit of happiness is not just a phrase in our founding document but a lived reality for all Americans.

The choice before us is clear: we can continue down the path of ever-expanding government control, inching closer to the communist-inspired C.F.S.M vision of a state-dominated society, or we can recommit ourselves in version 12.0 to the principles of limited government and individual liberty that have been the source of American greatness.

Let us choose wisely, for the future of our republic hangs in the balance. The task of shrinking government and defeating communist influence is not just a political imperative – it is a moral obligation we owe to ourselves, to our children, and to America.

It is time for U.S. – 12.0… an upgrade once again.

Chapter 2: Family – A Dying Breed

The family unit is the fundamental building block upon which communities, societies, and entire civilizations are constructed. It is within the family that individuals first learn about love, security, trust, responsibility, and the core values that shape their character and, later, their worldview. When families are strong, societies thrive. Conversely, when family structures break down, the repercussions can be felt throughout every level of society.

In a well-functioning family and even in many dysfunctional families, children are nurtured, protected, and guided. They learn essential life skills, develop emotional intelligence, and form their first social bonds - experiences that lay the groundwork for their future interactions with the broader world. As they grow, children who have benefited from stable family environments are more likely to become highly productive, well-adjusted and contributing members of society.

Moreover, families serve as a buffer against many of society's ills. Strong family units can provide emotional and financial support during times of hardship, reducing the burden on public resources as they act as the safety net. They also play a crucial role in transmitting cultural values and traditions from one generation to the next, ensuring the continuity and stability of society. Parental guidance is unique in its depth, continuity, and personalization. Parents have an intimate understanding of their children's personalities, strengths, and weaknesses, allowing them to tailor their advice and support in ways that other mentors or authority figures simply cannot match. The bond between parent and child creates a level of trust and openness that facilitates the transmission of not just information but also values, beliefs, and life skills, and it is being usurped.

Two-parent households offer several advantages, including diverse perspectives, shared responsibilities, financial stability, emotional support, and role modeling. Attempts to replace the traditional family structure, whether through government intervention or other societal arrangements, often fall short of providing these benefits and are at the core of what C.F.S.M communists wish to do to the family unit.

The government, no matter how well-intentioned, cannot replicate the personalized care, unconditional love, and nuanced guidance that parents provide. The government should only seek to aid those children who are most in need of physical stability and should seek to align with another family unit as soon as possible. The child is the focus, not the government.

Threats to the Family and the Role of Government:

The importance of the family unit in maintaining a free and prosperous society has not gone unnoticed by those who seek to fundamentally transform social structures. Particularly relevant is the relationship between communism and the family. For communism to survive, the family unit

MUST DIE, as stated previously…can't say it enough. The "Great Society" programs, initiated by President Lyndon B. Johnson in the mid-1960s, serve as a stark example of how perceptually well-intentioned government policies can have devastating unintended consequences and, in this case, on family structures. These welfare programs (economically called **transfer payments**), aimed at eliminating poverty and racial injustice, created financial incentives for massive expansion of single parenthood, leading to a sharp increase in single-parent households. This dramatic shift in family structure, especially in the black community and now in all, has been linked to a range of social issues, including higher poverty rates, lower educational attainment, and increased involvement in the criminal justice system.

The expansion of this government influence into traditionally familial domains represented a broader trend that extends beyond specific programs. These programs actively disincentivized fathers to remain in the family structure. Prior to this "Great Society" program, black families had 7+ out of 10 fathers in the household, and now the figure has sunk to 2-3 out of the same 10. There is something to be said about the leadership of a father, and when you remove it, you remove a pillar from the family foundation.

Active parenting serves as a bulwark against this expansion of state influence. When parents are deeply involved in their children's lives – educating them, instilling values, providing guidance and support – they naturally limit the need or opportunity for government intervention and are a direct attack against communism C.F.S.M forces. Active parenting also plays a crucial role in developing critical thinking skills, emotional resilience, and self-reliance – qualities that are antithetical to the dependency that communist systems often create.

The Culture War and Moral Values

The "culture war" refers to the ideological and cultural divide that exists within our society, encompassing a wide range of issues from family values and education to politics and religion. Cultural degradation, marked by the erosion of traditional values, the breakdown of social institutions, and the normalization of destructive behaviors, poses a significant threat to our families.

Policies that allow **minors** to make certain gender medical decisions without parental consent, the expansion of C.F.S.M public education, and the growth of various social services can all be seen as the government taking on roles traditionally filled by parents. This can weaken the bond between parent and child and reduce the role of parents in guiding their children's development.

Identifying signs of cultural degradation, such as the weakening of family structures, declining civic engagement, the loss of shared cultural narratives, increasing moral relativism, hyper-individualism, and the degradation of public discourse, is crucial. The effects of cultural degradation can be far-reaching, leading to social fragmentation, negative economic consequences, educational challenges at all levels, political instability and volatility, and mental health issues.

Addressing cultural degradation requires a multi-faceted approach:

- Strengthening families through taxation policies, not handouts
- Reforming the education system through parental choice
- Promoting civic involvement and discussion with shared American values
- Supporting moral and cultural institutions through education and patronage
- Addressing economic opportunities for new entrants
- Dramatically limiting and exposing Social Media's reach over minors with legal assistance

Protecting moral values is a crucial aspect of this effort, but it is a complex and often contentious issue. Moral values serve important functions, providing a framework for decision-making, creating social cohesion and trust, contributing to societal stability, and helping individuals find meaning and purpose.

Strategies for protecting moral values include, first and foremost, putting parents directly in front of the moral question, and if they disagree, then that would be 90% of the battle. Of course, there is education, leading by example, promoting civil discourse, supporting faith communities, responsible media, and supporting a legal framework that reflects and protects fundamental moral values while respecting individual rights. However, it begins with parental consent first because if the parent says no to something being taught, then all must abide by their wishes, end of story.

Balancing parental rights vs. individual choice and personal responsibility is essential, as is addressing specific cultural issues like gender, sexuality, education, media, technology, and religion in public life. **Let me be clear: the parent wins on all counts until the child is 18 or considered an adult. Family comes first.**

Protecting Children and Restoring Moral American Values

Traditional American values, such as individual liberty, limited government, free market capitalism, the rule of law, patriotism, a strong work ethic, and the importance of family, are all under threat. They all mean nothing if families cannot protect the innocence of their children. Addressing this challenge requires a multi-pronged approach:

Education CHOICE Reform: Incorporating civics and capitalist type education, character development, and critical thinking into school curricula… (To be expanded upon in Chapter 3) all based on parental choice.

Strengthening Families: Promoting marriage and family stability through tax policy changes, emphasizing parental responsibility, and supporting work-life balance are just scratching the surface. The potential removal of the child tax credit in favor of much lower taxes for families with children could greatly help stabilize the family unit, as in the long run, it will increase financial stability and lead to financial freedom.

While this change may negatively impact single-parent households, accommodations can be made. However, it is a step in the right direction to address this issue. Having both a mother and father in the household can greatly benefit families, and stabilizing them financially would be a positive first step. However, it's important to phase in this change gradually, as many single-parent households currently rely on government assistance, and a different structure will need to be created.

Even with 2-parent family homes, more are now a 2-parent working family household, and it has negatively impacted our children. We just don't have the same influence and time that we used to have. Nowadays, our children are left to the communist C.F.S.M wolves in education and online, who are confusing and manipulating them in ways most parents can't even fathom, to separate them from the family as they are "true believers."

This is akin to lions picking off the weak gazelle because they can't take down the rhino. As an example of this, recently, children were exposed to cross-dressing transvestites at an educational event IN SCHOOL, giving the minors sexual lap dances in blatant disregard for their minor status while onlookers clapped and cheered…really?

This is only one of many disgusting trends and debased acts against our children, and it is one of the prime reasons for undertaking this project. Not only should events like this never take place, but ALL the participants, down to the person who booked the call, should do time in prison, **NO EXCEPTIONS when it comes to protecting children's innocence.**

In the military, if something is objectionable in terms of an order being issued and you feel it is criminal, the right is on your side, and you can object to the order if you feel that a crime is being committed. The same should be true for any personnel who are involving themselves because the job is forcing them to do it, specifically in the sexualization of children in the education field. You must object and fight the immoral order or curriculum.

Civic Engagement: We all want to encourage voting, political participation, volunteerism, and involvement in local community organizations. At its core this alone could rectify the system if the system is perceived to be fair, but most people don't have the time to get involved as we are all working ridiculously long hours. Hence, we are partially to blame for not using the tools we already have in place; please get involved if you can.

Media and Cultural Initiatives: Supporting family-friendly entertainment, promoting media literacy with parent-approved books, and celebrating positive role models while safeguards are put in place for inappropriate content. Even PG movies somehow work in family objectionable material. We are all continually appalled at how much we must interact with all of these social media devices and networks to simply try to get decent content for our children.

The mental health issues faced by this generation due to the lack of fun and innocent social engagement is an epidemic worse than Covid. It correlates with the rise of cell phone addiction, and it will be a plague upon our society for many years to come. Numerous works have detailed this, and it has reached an epidemic crescendo. The Anxious Generation by Jonathan Haidt was particularly eye-opening and is a recommended read/listen.

Economic Family Friendly Policies: Implementing progressive taxation directly benefiting family units with children, strengthening labor protections for parents, and supporting entrepreneurship and small businesses for parents is a solid step in the right direction. We must reduce the financial fear for families as much as we can to encourage more family units to grow.

In subsequent chapters, this shortfall is addressed with the realization that the education system is most at fault for both the cultural rot and lack of small business development by many citizens. Small businesses create more jobs and opportunities and will cure many issues of economic inequality. Families today are facing increased pressure from large corporations, stifling opportunities for small businesses. This pattern must be reversed.

Legal and Political Reform to Benefit Families: Appointing or electing judges who respect the original intent of the Constitution and limiting government overreach. The founding fathers viewed the judicial branch as the branch potentially becoming the most problematic due to the power of activism on the bench. The recent demonstrations of lawfare conducted against our former president have completely undermined the legal system and have seriously diminished the respect that it needs to prevail and control our society. The Machiavellian approach of "getting" the former president at all costs will justify the means, which is exactly what we are all facing, and families will be next.

The process of **removing activist judges** should be simple and tied to local communities, as that's where the most damage is done. A straightforward formula based on overturned cases due to constitutional grounds should be the basis for removal. Just like every other individual, judges are human and susceptible to human frailties and insecurities. However, it's important to note that families feel the justice system is not protecting them and that they are on their own. This trend must be reversed.

Immigration and Assimilation of all New Families: Enforcing immigration laws, promoting shared values through assimilation, and celebrating legal immigration. The Sci-Fi "Borg," an alien species from Star Trek, seeks to incorporate the capabilities and expertise of other

UNITED STATES 12.0 – FREEDOM VS. COMMUNISM

civilizations into their own society through a process referred to as "assimilation" throughout the series. I firmly believe assimilation is necessary for America to thrive.

However, the forces of physical assimilation with the fictional Borg are without freedom and choice, making it a form of enslavement and a tool of the C.F.S.M communist. Immigrants who choose to come to the United States legally must assimilate to our ways by choice, and they must be free to make that commitment or leave. Without the choice, they become the Borg in the communist machine, which partially explains why our own government is allowing millions of illegal immigrants to flood and invade the system. They are physically committed to the generous benefits the U.S. offers, and the irony is that they think it is their choice, but it is not. Once the benefits are removed, true assimilation can begin as they must choose to align.

Ultimately, people who are illegal in the system have no choice but to conform to the communist leadership or face the consequences... What would you do? 9 out of 10 will probably take the money and run.

Our children ask about family history, and our continual answer should be that we are Americans. Yes, we appreciate the cultural distinctiveness of our European, African, Asian or any other ancestry and background, and yes, we appreciate many aspects of history, but our core is American.

Our grandparents and great-grandparents saw to it that their families would assimilate and become Americans and put behind them their traditions of the past, not forget, but put America first. English was force learned in less than 6 months, and everybody contributed to the family unit to survive.

Today, many new immigrants, especially illegal immigrants, struggle to understand the concept of loyalty and allegiance to the U.S., as they often hold on to their past while living in a new country. This is evident in various ways, which stems from their illegal entry in most cases. In contrast, legal immigrants are typically very pro-American, assimilate well, and contribute and add to the cultural mix from a family perspective.

Technological Responsibility to Protect Children: Protecting family, children, and individual privacy, promoting responsible technology use, and supporting innovation that is aligned with traditional values are crucial priorities. Privacy must be a central focus for all social media companies and technology providers. Safeguarding privacy is fundamental to preserving personal freedom. However, it is obvious that social media companies and the government do not and will not cooperate with privacy initiatives because they cut directly into advertising dollars and claimed security issues. This trend must be reversed and revised.

9-11-2001 changed how the government spied on its people as the intent was to root out terrorists with the passing of the "Patriot Act."

Like all tyrannical governments, they abused the trust that we gave them and turned these weapons on perceived enemies of the state. The Patriot Act and activist judges must be removed, and the spying and lawfare against American citizens must stop. Leadership at all levels of society, from political to community to cultural, is crucial in articulating and demonstrating these values. Measuring progress through indicators like civic engagement, family stability, education outcomes, economic metrics, and legal/political measures can help guide these efforts.

It is no secret that there is a dearth of leadership and experience, and we need new natural leaders steeped in Capitalist ways with solid moral compasses to help guide our constitutional republic, or it will end up in tyranny in the new "dark ages."

Economic Challenges Facing Families

The United States faces a range of significant economic challenges, including:

Wage Stagnation due in part to illegal immigration: The widening income inequality between the wealthy and the rest of the population, coupled with stagnant middle-class wages, presents challenges for social cohesion and economic opportunity. Corporations that are adept at navigating inflationary periods LOVE illegal immigration and can leverage their resources to maintain profitability, even as wage growth lags behind rising costs of living for families who are stuck in the middle. This dynamic erodes the purchasing power of the middle and lower economic classes. Addressing these imbalances is crucial if we aim to provide a better future for ourselves and our descendants.

Job Market Disruptions: Automation, the rise of the gig economy, and remote work are transforming the nature of work, requiring new approaches to workforce development. As a result, social safety nets are growing, which is what has led to more socialistic policies.

Technological innovation is a way of life as it increases productivity, but it can have destructive effects on families that are unable to adapt and change.

National Debt and Fiscal Responsibility: The growing national debt, with its potential to limit the government's ability to respond to future crises and burden future generations, necessitates a renewed focus on fiscal responsibility. Without trying to sound apocalyptic, we are headed for fiscal disaster.

To put it bluntly, we have severely hamstrung the government's ability to respond to emergencies, as interest payments on our towering debt have become the single largest budget item. Imagine a family that simply charges everything to credit cards without ever paying them back - the inevitable result is fiscal ruin and bankruptcy. And in this regard, the federal government is no different.

Healthcare Costs and New System Access: The high costs and uneven access to healthcare have significant economic implications, requiring reforms to address administrative complexity, drug prices, and the transition to value-based care.

UNITED STATES 12.0 – FREEDOM VS. COMMUNISM

One of the greatest expenses in a family's budget is STILL healthcare, and our approach to healthcare is nothing short of disastrous.

The answer to healthcare is market-based. It is not to expand the socialistic single-payer system but to increase the supply of doctors and access to them. Mandating families to purchase a centralized healthcare system can be equated to living in tyranny since you are removing choice from the equation.

So how do you do that?

We need to develop 2 systems… it is obvious that the communist forces will never stop, so a single-payer system will unfortunately continue to exist.

So, the way to achieve freedom for families is to allow them to choose from a newly established private market-based system with doctors at the center. Essentially, doctors should be allowed to become their own healthcare companies and offer unique plans, just like school choice would do. However, doctors who are not financially incentivized and protected from frivolous lawsuits will never participate in a market-based system.

Families need access to doctors and protection from frivolous lawsuits, and to that end, doctors need to become their own healthcare providers with their own individual plans that families can select based on their specific needs. It makes no sense to have Catholic nuns pay for abortion care, and trying to fit it all into one system is the problem.

Choice is the answer. The new market-based healthcare system must be decentralized and removed from government control in the newly developed mirror system. In this regard, many "efficiencies" will take place naturally as the costs decrease as the supply of doctors increases, and families will benefit by putting choice and freedom back into the equation.

By financially incentivizing doctors rather than incentivizing highly inefficient bureaucracy through a single-payer system, we'll keep the American healthcare system at the cutting edge of development and care and, at the same time, provide care to the poorest of our society. The overall supply of doctors will naturally increase due to the protections and financial incentives. This, in turn, will improve choice as families will have more to choose from and eventually, prices will equalize, and the system will be efficient.

Global Economic Competition – Do Families Need to Care?

Yes, families do need to care. The rise of China, India, and other emerging economies, trade imbalances, and intellectual property concerns put pressure on the United States to maintain its global competitiveness. On its face, it seems simple to fix, but the truth is we are better off developing fair trade than becoming what many people call protectionist and isolated since it increases the standard of living of families in the long run. The key is fairness and honesty. China has proven itself to be an unfair and dishonest trading partner and isn't the only one. Therefore, we need **protective tariffs** to safeguard our interests. In a purely academic, "ceteris paribus" (all things being equal) economic world, protectionism is bad, but in reality, it is necessary as all countries are not equal, and especially for bad actors like China that disregard out intellectual property.

However, there are far-reaching consequences to these global imbalances, and it is not just financial. By shifting from a manufacturing society to a service-based economy, we have also changed the gender dynamic in our country, which has led to many cultural issues.

The traditional roles of the man in the family were based largely on strength from the past, which stemmed from a manufacturing society. In a service-based economy, strength is almost irrelevant, and the cultural wars bear that out by denigrating the masculinity of men in many cases in favor of forced equality, a totally unnecessary fight as it is a natural progression and perfectly fine competition.

The new service-based economy offers tremendous opportunities as it levels the work playing field between men and women. The changing roles of fathers and mothers due to work changes is a dynamic that we will all have to learn to adapt to keep our families together. Ultimately, we need to find a solid balance between manufacturing and service economies and, at the same time, stop attacking each other and protective tariffs can help us in the short term.

Environmental Challenges and Family War with The Green Economy:

Climate change is, of course, a necessary part of life as the climate is always changing; however, using the climate for political gain should be exposed and rejected. The market distortions created by this government-created hysteria are particularly damaging to families who rely upon low-cost energy to survive. Higher fuel costs lead to all types of **negative externalities**, such as higher costs and food due to transportation costs rising, heating one's home, commuting to your job, and a host of other smaller indirect costs directly impacting the survivability of families.

With conflicting scientific viewpoints and sensationalistic claims, family's purchasing decisions are all in the crosshairs of this largely politically motivated movement. Yes, humans can affect pollution, and yes, we must all care about it, but to attribute planetary climate change to humans without looking at every possible scenario is ludicrous.

A potential irony is that we are at the end of a 206-year cycle and are headed into a solar cooling phase, not the heating phase that is often discussed. This cooling trend is a topic that is explored in depth in the book "Dark Winter," which is a well-researched and scientifically grounded read.

This type of fantastic sensationalism would be completely averted if politicians had more private sector experience, which is one of the tenets of this book. When you couple these claims with a lack of trust in leaders, it's no wonder families are fragmented on this topic.

Small Businesses and Entrepreneurship: The unique challenges facing small businesses and startups, from access to capital to regulatory burdens, limit most family's ability to drive innovation and job creation.

Many families are stagnating due to economic malaise and the complexity and financial burden of starting a new business. Most do not take the initiative to start a new venture out of fear of losing everything they have. It's important to note that the communist C.F.S.M. does not support the growth of small businesses because it believes that doing so would lead to increased financial independence and stronger family units. Instead, the communist agenda aims to bolster large businesses while subjugating and subordinating small businesses, effectively wiping out the middle.

In the next chapter on education, we will take a deeper dive into the topic of entrepreneurship and private sector experience for politicians and discuss why both the education system and politicians, in general, have also fallen short in this area. Ultimately, providing easier access to capital and reducing the risk of financial collapse would lead to a significant expansion of entrepreneurship - something we have not seen in a very long time.

Housing Affordability and Homelessness: The lack of affordable housing in many areas of the country has significant economic and social consequences for our citizens. Policy interventions to increase supply and protect vulnerable populations. Undoubtedly, a sudden influx of 20 million new residents without adequate housing infrastructure would be a recipe for catastrophic consequences. Immigrants, in general, tend to occupy the lower rungs of the housing ladder, given their limited options. This, in turn, triggers a domino effect, pushing moderate-income families to seek mid-range accommodations and the middle class to vie for high-end properties, resulting in a nationwide surge in both rental and home prices and subsequent shortages.

However, the solution lies not just in restrictive immigration policies but in the strategic expansion of tax and entrepreneurship programs for family units. We need to **remove all the individual minority focused business incentive programs and put family-centric business incentives** especially targeted at creating new housing. Families come in all varieties and this approach will go a long way to eliminate "victimization". This approach will dramatically increase the supply of housing because families are incentivized to create small businesses and build them.

By empowering families to establish their own construction businesses, we can catalyze a private-sector-driven response to the housing shortage rather than solely relying on government intervention.

The government's attempts to subsidize housing costs have inadvertently created a two-tiered market, further exacerbating the issue. In the past four years, rents have doubled in many areas directly due to government intervention, compelling private landlords to seek government subsidies and thus contributing to the inflationary pressures plaguing our society.

The black hole of government money never seems to stop and like black holes in space, sucks everything into them. Ultimately, it is the families who bear the brunt of this crisis, as their budgets are stretched to the limit, and their options to move multiple people at once are also limited, leaving them with little discretionary income to enjoy life's simple pleasures. How many American families are stuck in poor housing conditions due to this debacle?

New Educational Shift and Workforce Development: Ensuring a well-educated and skilled workforce is crucial for long-term economic success, so necessitating A complete overhaul to K-12 education (more to follow in next chapter), improving college affordability by removing the federal government from college, as much as possible, as all the federal dollars inflate the college bureaucracy. There must also be a massive expansion of vocational and business training at all levels.

However, it is very important to note that education by itself is clearly not the answer, to quote Calvin Coolidge, "The world is full of **educated derelicts**." This has led to the formation of a class known as the academic elite, which is essentially good for little else, as they aren't grounded and produce nothing of merit other than activist opinions. Education without action is useless. How many people do you know who have advanced degrees who do nothing of consequence with them?

The second half of the quote from Coolidge is that "The only thing in this world that truly matters is **perseverance**" when it comes to work ethic and economic development, as without it, you have a generation full of quitters and "victims." When you couple perseverance with freedom, stability, opportunity and choice, you have the most powerful combination to eliminate poverty and advance humanity. People feeling virtually limitless in their ability to achieve is what should be at the core of the economic development of families.

Infrastructure Investment: Modernizing and expanding America's aging infrastructure is ongoing and essential for enhancing economic productivity and competitiveness. The expansion of infrastructure is always necessary from a government perspective as it's very difficult for an individual to build a highway or bridge, and so the larger programs help expand entrepreneurship and, in essence, family development. This type of **fiscal** government spending should be the only type of fiscal government spending that we focus on in the next few decades, as it will lead to the support structure of developing good, solid families through empowered business opportunities.

Addressing these complex, interconnected challenges requires a comprehensive, balanced approach that involves bipartisan cooperation from new and **private sector experienced politicians**, long-term thinking, and a willingness to make difficult choices such as hypothetically increasing the Social Security age by one month per year for the next 15 years, and reducing transfer payments on a massive scale, and many other policy changes/reductions. Successful implementation will depend on strengthening new American Leadership with new innovative risk-takers. Promoting social cohesion by doing away with divisive programs such as DEI without merit and upholding the moral values that have long defined the nation.

America's Role in a Multipolar World – What do Families need to know?

The global landscape is always shifting to a more complex, multipolar world order. The rise of China as a global power and the resurgence of great power competition poses unique challenges for American leadership. It is important to note that trade is good and not evil, but trade must be fair.

The ascendance of China represents a significant challenge as Beijing seeks to reshape the global order in its image and has a long-term plan for global domination by the year 2049 (100 years after the communist party formed).

The future of U.S.-China relations will likely define much of the 21st century, requiring a delicate balance of pushing back against China's more aggressive actions while also finding areas for cooperation on global family issues, as the people of China are no different than families of the U.S. in that they all want the same things for their families. The difference between the two countries is in their governments as China is a communist regime where freedom and choice of the individual are removed from the equation without regard for liberty or religious freedom. China is very clear about this with numerous complaints levied against them.

Where the similarity lies now is that we are heading down a similar path, except we don't explicitly label it as communism. We are still in the process of naming the removal of our rights under a C.F.S.M agenda. One day, the people of China and the people of the United States will live in absolute harmony if both can put the family unit first and remove the C.F.S.M trend from the equation.

The resurgence of great power competition, with Russia, India, and the European Union also asserting their influence, underscores the continued importance of America's alliance system and Capitalist leadership. Strengthening ties with traditional allies and cultivating new partnerships will be crucial for maintaining influence and counterbalancing potential adversaries.

The revival of communist C.F.S.M powers is a recurring phenomenon, like climate cycles. We find ourselves once again battling against tyranny, as evil never seems to take a break. Our hope lies in learning from the mistakes that led to the Roman Empire's downfall to avoid plunging into another dark age.

China isn't the only nation that restricts the rights of its people; many countries do the same. This is why the United States and our Constitution should stand as a shining

UNITED STATES 12.0 – FREEDOM VS. COMMUNISM

example for the world. At our core, we value liberty and choice, which serve as powerful tools against our adversaries, as Ronald Reagan noted in his inaugural address in 1981. He emphasized that above all, we seek peace, and I believe this is true; peaceful people consider war a last resort. In contrast, communists act like bullies, often resorting to force, something we're witnessing in our own country today.

Regrettably, social media has become a tool for mass control rather than an ally. It has become the latest weapon in the communist C.F.S.M arsenal, one they are effectively wielding and right under our collective noses. The destructive impact of social media on families highlights the urgent need to prioritize privacy and strengthen family units in any future reforms. For families to thrive, the era of social media dominance must come to an end, and parents must have a fast-track, empowered way to sue and attack these companies on behalf of their children and families.

The competition of ideas in the digital age, with the liberal democratic model championed by the United States, facing challenges from authoritarian regimes and populist movements, has become a critical battleground. The United States must grapple with how to promote free expression and the open exchange of ideas online while also countering disinformation and protecting democratic processes and intellectual copyrights and patents.

Redefining American exceptionalism to emphasize the nation's capacity for reinvention, commitment to freedom and democratic values, and ability to bring diverse peoples and ideas together is the way forward by focusing on families first.

Investing in domestic strengths, bridging internal divisions, and embracing a more collaborative approach to US leadership principles will be key to maintaining American influence and shaping a more stable, prosperous, and just international order. America is still the shining city on the hill as Ronald Reagan put it, and we must always trust that individual freedom and liberty is the way to strengthen families.

Transitioning to a clean energy economy in an American family friendly fashion is undoubtedly one of the greatest challenges facing our planet, as it directly impacts the lower echelons of the economic spectrum and devastates family's discretionary money. This transition, however, should **not be** mandated but rather driven by incentives for clean energy adoption and a just transition for fossil fuel-dependent communities.

The most abundant element in the universe, hydrogen, has already been developed into a clean-burning, low-cost energy source with immense potential for long-term expansion. By harnessing the power of hydrogen, we can set the stage for the most massive economic expansion in human history, where the standard of living for the bottom 40% of the planet will increase almost instantaneously, and that alone will strengthen all family units. Reimagining transportation and urban planning, building resilience to climate impacts, and driving global action through innovation and technology are essential elements of this response. However, **we must move away from the obsessive battery-driven focus,** as it too has the potential for long-term economic damage to the planet with aggressive lithium mining.

Elon Musk's ideas and work are awesome. They should not be mandated, as they do little to help families now and drive up the costs of government incentives and programs, further exacerbating the inflation and resource allocation problems.

Fostering a new American mission centered on US global leadership can reinvigorate the economy, reassert American values, and forge a better future for all families. The reason much of the world wants to emigrate to the United States is not accidental – it is a testament to the enduring appeal of American family ideals and the promise of opportunity.

When you ask any immigrant why they left their country, they will likely say that they wanted a better life for themselves and their children. Most of them are not fleeing political oppression but rather are escaping from bad economic systems and corrupt leaders in their home countries, seeking better opportunities elsewhere, and none of those countries should receive any US financial aid until they change their economic systems. This transition, however, will require sustained political will, significant investment, and a willingness to make difficult choices. The choices made in the coming years will determine not just the future of the United States but the future of the planet and the survivability of the family structure for generations to come in every country, not just the United States.

Chapter 3: Public and Private Education and Parental Choice

The public education system in its current state is **severely flawed** and unlikely to improve in the foreseeable future. This system, which was largely shaped by John Rockefeller in the early 20th century, was not designed to foster critical thinking, creativity, and independent learning – the very skills needed to thrive in the modern world. Rather, it was intentionally structured to **produce obedient, compliant workers** to serve the interests of industry and the established social order, and it hasn't changed since.

Rockefeller's million-dollar initial donation in 1902, equivalent to around $40 million today, was pivotal in cementing the model of public education that we still see today. He made it clear from the outset that his vision was not to cultivate free-thinkers and entrepreneurs but to create a **docile workforce** that could perform basic functional tasks without question. This aligned with the needs of the industrialized economy at the time, which valued efficiency and uniformity over individualism and innovation and funneled in much more money along the way.

As the decades passed, more and more public funding was poured into this bad system, further entrenching the Rockefeller control model. The public education system became the most effective tool for controlling and assimilating the masses of both new immigrants and existing citizens by indoctrinating them through schools. The current education system has a myriad of flaws and typically follows a narrow, standardized curriculum, which still discourages critical analysis of the status quo. **It can be seen as more oppressive than the U.S. prison system, trapping young minds in a cycle of conformity and undermining their natural curiosity and desire to learn.**

While not all institutions exhibit these exact characteristics, many do because they prioritize financial gains to keep the bureaucratic machine funded. During the COVID lockdown, so many parents were disillusioned and disgusted by the strong-arm tactics of the school boards and administrators who were getting their marching orders directly from communist C.F.S.M central state leadership. Like good C.F.S.M communists, they obeyed because they dangled the money in front of them - a tried-and-true tactic to keep administrators in line.

Lack Of Socialization Skills

There is a stark contrast between the amount of playtime afforded to schoolchildren versus incarcerated individuals in prisons and is a startling indictment of the priorities and failings of the modern public education system.

As highlighted in Jonathan Haidt's book "The Anxious Generation," children today spend less than an hour per day engaged in play and social interaction, while even **prisoners** are granted a more generous two hours of such activities. When prisoners were asked how they would react if their allotted playtime was cut down to just one hour per day, their response was unequivocal: they predicted widespread riots across the country. This powerful illustration underscores the fundamental human need for social engagement, physical activity, and unstructured exploration – needs that are being systematically neglected in the current educational paradigm and then cemented into stone, further isolating our kids with addiction to phones and social media apps.

The modern phenomenon of school shootings always comes down to disconnected individuals from society. Clearly, some are more disconnected than others, but when you point out the lack of socialization time in schools coupled with a lack of innovative curriculums that aren't focused on real economics, it is no wonder that individuals lose their way and lose a sense of purpose toward the greater human good.

By engaging students in more interactive, fun, and educational activities, we can help develop better-grounded individuals and, as a result, stronger families.

WE WANT TO CONNECT as kids, and if we don't do it as kids, the task becomes harder and harder as adults.

Horace Mann is often credited as the architect of the modern public education system, but in reality, the system as we know it today was largely shaped by the influence and money of John Rockefeller in the early 20th century.

While Horace Mann may have been a sincere advocate for expanding educational opportunities and creating a more informed citizenry, the Rockefeller model that ultimately prevailed prioritized conformity and compliance over the holistic nurturing of young minds; this legacy continues to haunt the public education system, which often feels more akin to a prison than a place of learning and growth. Is it any wonder that kids become more and more disconnected?

This neglect of the fundamental human needs of children is not only detrimental to their physical and mental well-being but also stifles their innate curiosity, creativity, and problem-solving abilities – the very skills that will be essential for them to thrive in the rapidly changing world they will inherit.

When you couple this with the immoral and, quite frankly, disgusting movement to allow immature, lonely and troubled children to mutilate themselves, it is no wonder this is the most confused generation to walk this Earth. What implications does this have for the next 100 years?

To truly transform the public education system and better serve the needs of students, we must be willing to challenge the Rockefeller model immediately and begin with its underlying assumptions.

This will require a free rethinking of the purpose of education, with a renewed emphasis on personalized, student-centered learning and a commitment to nurturing the holistic development of young minds – including the critical role of play, social interaction, and exploration, and always it begins with money, or should I say the choice and money. Only by breaking free from the constraining legacy of the Rockefeller model can we create an education system that truly empowers and inspires the next generation, equipping them with the tools and mindset to navigate the complexities of the 21st century and shape a better future for all.

A Suffocating Bureaucratic Behemoth– K-12 Public Education

Most young college students who endeavor to become teachers are usually very motivated in their early years. In many cases, they are placed in very difficult assignments, which is almost akin to hazing, as every senior teacher in the school knows what the good and bad assignments are.

And so, they look at it as a rite of passage and throw the young teachers into the deep end of the pool without any swimming lessons. Many of these new teachers should simply "apprentice teach" for years with different teachers until they are ready…a possible simple fix.

The initial enthusiasm of young teachers diminishes as they are burdened with administrative work instead of focusing on teaching and connecting with their students. Their new ideas are often suppressed, leading to a loss of motivation. As a result, many leave the profession early because they feel their creativity and nurturing instincts are stifled in a bureaucratic system.

Despite the astronomical sums we pour into education - close to $37,000 (and counting) per student on average in New York – the academic results are no better than much of the globe. We are one of the highest-taxed states in the country, yet our educational outcomes remain woefully mediocre, and many blue states are in the same position, as these states are in a communist C.F.S.M model of tyrannical control via unions and bureaucrats. The stranglehold on the process will not be conquered from the outside and must be attacked at the micro level by **parental choice.**

How Do We Change This Obsolete System?

There is no one silver bullet that will fix this. However, we must act and prioritize a human-centric approach over an academic one when evaluating progress. This shift in thinking has the potential to revolutionize education as we know it and, more importantly, strengthen family bonds, ultimately leading to the development of more productive and purposeful children who will be better equipped to lead the next generation. How can we make this happen?

Public schooling must always remain an option, but the funding structure needs a complete reevaluation, and it begins with parents. **Parents must be empowered to direct the resources toward the educational paths they deem most suitable for their children** - be it private schools, religious institutions, homeschooling, or alternative online options. A 75/25 split is more than adequate, with 75% of the funds under parental control and 25% retained for essential services and special needs, which would be a game-changing shift. This freedom to choose to restructure would not only restore parental agency but would also serve as a potent check on the systemic activism that has plagued our schools and communities via the C.F.S.M communist.

An Efficiency Revolution in Education

As parents **redirect** their financial support, the bloated administrative apparatus would be forced to naturally downsize, and the schools would become much leaner overnight and more responsive to the needs of the family and community. This "Pareto Optimal" (Economist Vilfredo Pareto) effect is the first step to fixing the system…**parents control the money**, not the C.F.S.M communist. The idea or concept is to make both parties better off with a single decision, akin to the proverbial "killing two birds with one stone."

It's time to dismantle the broken system and pave the way for a new, truly empowered, and innovative era of education with merit and choice leading the way and beginning from the bottom up, not the top down. By putting the control into the hands of the parents, we empower the parents to make the best decisions for their families with their priorities, not the state's edicts.

Potential Ideas and Outcomes: Restructured School Days and Calendar

The typical school day runs from around 6-7 am to 5 pm, with students spending approximately 8 hours of this time in the school environment and the rest on transportation. This lengthy and inflexible schedule does not align with the natural rhythms and attention spans of young learners. Students often become fatigued and disengaged during the latter half of the day, limiting the effectiveness of instruction in this prison model. It should be noted that the typical school day mirrored the schedule for factory workers in an industrialized economy, which is exactly what Rockefeller wanted. As an added benefit to the communist C.F.S.M model, if students don't like the factory schedule and turn to a life of crime, it is good news for them since the schedule is the same as the prison schedule and allows for an easier transition to prison life!

See? They really do have a choice! The biggest misunderstanding is that we are no longer in a 100% industrialized economy; we are in a mixed entrepreneurial, industrialized and mostly service-based economy with very flexible schedules. This alone should be the impetus to allow flexibility and change.

Concurrently, the current school calendar also includes an unusually long summer break of 13 weeks, as well as extensive time off for holidays like Christmas and Easter. When you couple this with numerous teachers checking out early in May and June with movies in the classroom and lots and lots of "tests." This extended time away from actual learning can and does lead to significant **learning loss** and tremendous **learning gaps**, particularly for students from disadvantaged backgrounds. The long gaps in instruction make it challenging for good teachers to maintain continuity and momentum in their lessons and curriculum. As a result, they have to scaffold back numerous times. When you factor in being placed with different teachers all the time, it isn't hard to see why so many cracks exist in the system. It also explains why our children get lost and end up in the world of social media debauchery. On average, less than 2 hours a day is attributed to actual learning in the class; the rest is all fluff and obedience, and that is at the decent schools. The rest of the day is filled with conformity and pecking order issues.

Is it any wonder that many of today's modern students are disillusioned with this model and gravitate to isolation?

To fix this issue, it won't happen from the top down because the communist bureaucratic regime has too much control. The only way to fix this is through the creation of new schools with innovative teachers, not just administrators who understand the importance of this.

A myriad of factors must take place in order for change to occur, as families have become far too complacent in using schools as daycare so that they can work. We can't blame parents for this because they're stretched so far economically that they have no choice. The two functions must be separated.

Schools have also been more than happy to accept the increased indoctrination time by offering even more welfare benefits such as food and additional daycare services, and the list goes on and on. So, in an ideal world, what would new places of learning look like?

- Shorter, flexible school days with year-round learning
- Decoupling of welfare and academics

- Increased focus on competitive academics, socialization and fun events
- Individualized targeted learning extended to all students
- Strict ban on cell phone usage in school

The only way that this could begin to take shape is through a completely decentralized model, which is where parental choice comes into play. **In the same way that we advocate for doctors as the center of the model to fix the healthcare system, we advocate for teachers, not administrators, to have the power to create their own schools and learning environments in this new type of flexible model**. Too many times, good teachers are stifled from doing the things that they know would work because of the bureaucratic communist system that is presently in place.

This type of new school slash entrepreneurial business model would be funded by parents who choose to send their kids to these new, fun and unique institutions, thus creating a revolution in education, all based on parental choice and empowerment, while concurrently dismantling the communist C.F.S.M. System. The public education system should move away from the prison-like model and instead adopt a more flexible approach with shorter school days, approximately 4-5 hours a day, and much fewer non-teaching administrators. Shorter days but longer periods of instruction throughout the year would help students maintain focus and engagement while reducing significant gaps in learning. This new model would also allow for increased social engagement and enable teachers to focus on teaching and facilitating rather than acting as babysitters or social workers.

The public education system needs to decouple completely from the welfare system. The two should not be linked just because it is convenient. The programs must be kept separate.

"Communist/Marxist" C.F.S.M Model and Replacing Parents

The flawed "communist/Marxist" C.F.S.M model that seeks to replace the role of parents and family attempts to act as a child's "mother and father," providing not just academic instruction but also social, emotional, and even moral guidance. It is truly Orwellian. It was one of the main reasons to add more welfare-type services into the education model to make it easier to be a "Big Daddy Government."

This massive overreach of the government's authority clearly undermines the fundamental role of the family in a free society, as mentioned in Chapter 3, and just about everywhere. The current public education system is **not** aligned with the values and principles of a "free-thinking, capitalistic society." By continued emphasis on conformity, standardization, and state control, which all stifles the entrepreneurial spirit and independent thinking essential for success in a competitive, market-driven economy, the current system is a failure in epic proportions.

A New Education Model With Technology and Adaptive Learning at Its Core

To assist new schools and teachers and in response to these multipronged shortcomings, education reform calls for a new model that leverages **technology and adaptive learning** to better meet the needs of modern students and prepare them for the challenges of the 21st century. Several educational technology companies have already developed innovative approaches to learning that utilize adaptive and scaffolding models.

These individual adaptive and interactive models allow students to progress at their own pace, with the curriculum and instructional materials tailored to their individual needs and learning styles. This can lead to exponential gains in student achievement, as each student is able to focus on the areas where they need the most support with facilitation and instruction by motivated teachers.

By leveraging technology and adaptive learning, students can learn at a much faster and more efficient rate than in the traditional, one-size-fits-all classroom model. This can lead to significant academic growth and better prepare students for the demands of the modern workforce and economy. In this new education model, teachers would transition from the role of lecturer and caregiver to that of learning facilitator. Instead of simply delivering content, teachers would guide students through the learning process, helping them to navigate the adaptive curriculum, ask questions, and engage in hands-on, project-based learning activities. This model will allow teachers to become much more efficient and much better at their jobs of inspiring children to learn more. This type of focus will also allow one teacher to handle many more students, which will also alleviate overpopulation burdens in the education system, all while making the entire system more cost and educationally responsive and interesting to the student. All of this will lead to a renewed sense of purpose with students with families at the core.

In addition to the cell phone ban in class, the proposed education reform model calls for a significant increase in the amount of time dedicated to **social play and team-building** activities.

Rather than the current conformity model, which often relegates physical education and recess to the periphery, the new approach would dedicate four to five times more time to these crucial components of child social development.

These social play and team-building activities would be facilitated by FUN teaching professionals rather than administrators. The goal would be to create a more dynamic, engaging, and collaborative environment that fosters the development of important skills like teamwork, communication, and problem-solving through actual competitions.

A Possible Example

As part of this emphasis on social play and interaction, the expansion of intramural activities where students would be randomly assigned to three-person teams (need an odd number) that would rotate monthly; these monthly teams would compete in a variety of activities such as:

- academic challenges,
- debates,
- games,
- sports,
- business,
- civics,
- community-oriented projects and many more

The aim is to promote a sense of **healthy competition** while also cultivating **entrepreneurial spirit** and a stronger social connection to the broader community. This would be at the beginning or end of every day, and parents would or could participate if they wanted as role models. Can you imagine a day that starts with friends, family and playing but is actually a planned learning day with the intent of developing a competitive American spirit? It may even be acceptable to begin **and** end the day in the same way.

Now, that's something all families can engage in!

Learning and achievement will explode in the right direction and, more importantly, keep the family in the center of the day. Anxiety will diminish, and our children's lives will flourish. One of the key principles underlying this approach is **rejecting** the "everyone gets a trophy" mentality that has become prevalent in many schools and communities. While the focus would be on promoting teamwork and collaboration, the new model would also place a greater value on winning and achievement through teamwork and acceptance in a variety of academic and sport-type activities that all can participate in.

Losing is part of life, and we all know that it isn't how many times you get knocked down but how many times you get back up to try again. That is actually paraphrased from one of the Rocky movies, but the sentiment is real.

This would instill a sense of the importance of excellence and hard work while still maintaining a supportive, accepting environment in which children can thrive and achieve.

Equal time learning, playing and applying = purpose and lifelong trusted relationships.

Growing Entrepreneurial Skills and Mindsets

A key component of the proposed education reform is a greater emphasis on developing entrepreneurial skills and mindsets as part of the competitions. This would involve incorporating more instruction in areas like business planning, financial literacy, and innovative problem-solving at extremely young ages and something many parents could participate in. The goal is to cultivate a new generation of students who are better equipped to create their own economic opportunities and contribute to the overall vitality of the free-market system, and create businesses while in school.

This education reform model argues that by fostering stronger entrepreneurial skills and mindsets, the public education system can help promote greater family and societal stabilization and interactions, which will have tremendous long-term benefits for all.

Students who are able to achieve economic success and self-sufficiency will be less reliant on government assistance, have a higher moral sense of purpose, and are more likely to contribute to the overall well-being of their communities.

Greater participation amongst all students will lead to far fewer school shooting incidents and much stronger communities and families.

Elevating Roles of Teachers and Diminishing Roles of Administrators

While the proposed education reform model emphasizes the structural importance of technology and adaptive learning, it also calls for significant changes to the roles and responsibilities of teachers and administrators within the public education system. One of the key elements of the proposed reform is to give parents more control over the education funds that are allocated to their children's schools. This choice will help to address the issue of poor-performing teachers by empowering parents to remove their children from the classroom and school if so desired, with no repercussions at any time during the year.

This core tenant of reform alone will dramatically change the face of education; if it does not occur, then parents will have to contend with continued fighting with the communist C.F.S.M bureaucratic machine forever. It is a main contention of this book that financial control by the parent will automatically rectify everything that is wrong in the system, and from a politician's standpoint, it is the simplest of all fixes.

Additionally, proponents of the reform model believe that parents should have a much greater ability to remove teachers who engage in what they perceive as "social/activist" behavior, which they view as undermining the traditional values and priorities of their families and the education system. To this end, ALL school boards should ONLY consist of parents who have children in the CURRENT school system. Nobody will be more focused than a parent with a child at stake. Once their child leaves the school, the parent must exit the board.

From an efficiency and resource allocation standpoint, many poor teachers will leave the system as they will be exposed, and that will result in many good teachers/facilitators being paid more than they deserve. A system of **merit-based** pay will become more and more efficient. The proposed education reform model also calls for a significant reduction in the number of administrators within the public education system. Most administrative roles have been unnecessary for many years due to advancements in technology. The resources currently dedicated to these positions would be better utilized in direct support of student learning and instruction. The administrators and the bureaucrats currently in place are the gatekeeps and tools of the communist top-down approach and will fight to the death for their survival in the party, which is why it is advocated that parents **must control the purse strings**, which will immediately rectify this bloated system.

In the various new structures created, the remaining administrators would be recast as "facilitators" who work directly with students and teachers to support the learning process rather than engaging in bureaucratic tasks and decision-making and, most importantly, would report to the teachers.

Today's typical bureaucrat deals predominantly with complaints due to the inefficiencies of the system. It is hard to fathom a more useless position in society. In no way, shape or form do communist C.F.S.M bureaucrats help propel human beings to move forward or solve the complex problems we face. **No C.F.S.M bureaucrat should ever be paid more than the lowest teacher in the system**. By empowering parents to control the 75% bulk of education tax dollars, they can choose which school will best educate their child and enhance the **American Family Experience**. Efficiency will immediately follow as waste will melt from the system, as there won't be any place for poor teachers and

UNITED STATES 12.0 – FREEDOM VS. COMMUNISM

overpaid administrators to hide. Choice is everything to the family.

Teachers who truly value teaching and learning will love this freedom, flexibility and creativity in the new system, but teachers who are in it for the paycheck, who simply toe the line, or are trying to become a communist C.F.S.M bureaucrat will absolutely detest it and hide behind the union and resist. It is critical to emphasize that the winner in this entire equation is the **student**, then the **family**, then the **community** and, of course, our **country**. Conversely, the loser is the C.F.S.M communist.

- Destructive Social Media
- Privacy
- Sexualization of Children
- Cell Phone Addiction

All of the above are interlinked in varying degrees, just as C.F.S.M are all interlinked today, and all must be addressed as families every day are decimated by one or all with children who are detached, suicidal, lonely and scared. It is the saddest truth of our time, and no family is immune to it. The ubiquitous rise of social media and widespread cell phone addiction among the younger generation has become a mental health epidemic and a significant concern for many educators and, clearly, most parents. The evidence suggests that these technologies are having a profoundly negative impact, especially on young girls, but boys are right behind. The anecdotal evidence suggests that increased social media and cell phone addiction are linked to higher levels of anxiety, isolation, depression, suicides, disconnection, and the sexualization of children.

How much of these plays into school shootings is unknown and almost impossible to factor, but how can any sane person dismiss the obvious connections?

The impact on the mental health and well-being of the younger generation, as previously stated, is particularly alarming. Frequent social media addiction has also been correlated with poor sleep quality, low self-esteem, and a higher risk of developing eating disorders and body image issues. This is especially true for young girls, who are bombarded with unrealistic beauty standards and the constant pressure to present a curated, idealized version of their lives online. In response to these concerning trends, schools need to take a more proactive approach to address the challenges posed by destructive social media and cell phones. One of the key recommendations is to implement a complete ban on cell phone usage during school hours and, at the same time, massively increase human-to-human time through more fun gaming competitions.

To enforce this policy, schools would be required to first get parental approval and then provide lockboxes or other secure storage solutions where students would be required to store their phones upon arrival. This would ensure that students are not constantly distracted by notifications, social media updates, and the temptation to engage with their devices during learning time. Technology is constantly evolving to the point where phones can be carried but only have emergency call functionality during the entire day.

Parents will have to decide what is best for their child's school, but the damage to children from the use far outweighs the security concern argument.

With all of the negative effects mentioned, the **sexualization of children** in schools and in social media is deeply troubling and probably the most severely debilitating to our children. Children and adolescents are exposed to explicit content and predatory behavior at an extremely young age, with serious implications for their emotional and psychological development. This can and has led to premature sexual activity, increased vulnerability to exploitation, and a distorted understanding of healthy relationships.

There is an alarming and common-sense correlation between the rise of child sexualization and the increased use of drugs and morally bankrupt social media platforms accessed via devices, primarily phones. It is as if hunting season has opened for child predators on innocent children, and they are having a field day picking off the weak ones. To compound the problem, we have a government that is enabling these predators, or should just say animals, to further confuse children about thinking who and what they really are versus simply engaging, learning, and playing with appropriate trusted friends. It is as if the entire world, specifically America, has lost its collective mind.

Children are our most precious resource, and anyone who preys upon them should have the most severe penalties exacted upon them. The same goes for anyone who doesn't protect our children and that includes any educator or politician.

Schools should be safe places for learning and to make trusted friends. They should be places where children should ask themselves tough questions and try to get honest answers while they search for their place in our global society.

School should not be a place where social activists hide and breed. It should never be an extended babysitting or welfare program. Schools should not force learning, as learning should be fun and self-paced. Every single student should have an individual learning plan that fills every educational gap. It should be possible to have 9-year-olds competing blindly with 15-year-olds in subjects of strength. Conversely, the same 15-year-old can comfortably identify the gaps in their education and address them without being humiliated in front of classmates. I can only imagine how many school shooters felt alienated in some capacity for that exact reason.

In the current system, very few of these changes will be implemented as they are contrary to the interests of the communist C.F.S.M bureaucrat model. This is why school choice must be at the core and controlled by the parent and the parent alone. But what should we do if a parent refuses to participate in their child's education? Regardless of their race or gender, the school's parent board should take the first step in trying to help the disengaged parent. If they are unable to make the parent understand the importance of their involvement, then social services may need to get involved. However, this topic is beyond the scope of this book and it is what the remaining 25% in education will have to cover.

The current system is ripe with pedophiles and deviants, as they have all been given the green light by the C.F.S.M communists to destroy the family culture at will by indoctrinating and sexualizing children.

The time has never been clearer for parents to fight back and take back control of their families, their children's education, their communities, and their lives.

While the **death penalty** may seem overly harsh for many crimes, the exploitation and abuse of children is a uniquely abhorrent act that society should not tolerate. Those who prey on the innocence of young, vulnerable victims and inflict lasting psychological trauma deserve the most severe legal penalties. Our justice system needs to impose the strictest possible sentences for such predatory crimes against children. These types of offenders, who target innocent schoolchildren, should face the harshest societal condemnation and consequences…

Death is adequate but is probably too light a penalty for these crimes.

Curriculum Flexibility for Good Teachers

Lastly, the proposed reforms to social media and cell phone policies, as well as the emphasis on social play, competition and team building, are intended to address some of the more immediate challenges facing families and schools; there are also concerns about the broader curriculum and its perceived shift towards a "Marxist" C.F.S.M educational system.

In the current model, there has been a troubling trend toward eliminating the focus on capitalism, civics, historical patriotism, and our constitutional republic. They contend that this shift is part of a broader effort to create "useful idiots," as Lenin put it, who are more receptive to communist and socialist C.F.S.M ideologies to become activists as young as possible, just look at the misguided actions of the hate group ANTIFA. The ironic title is that it purports Anti-Fascism, hence the name "ANTIFA." These violent and misguided souls are Lenin's "useful idiots" who don't know that true fascism today lies in the collusion between government power and the influence of big tech companies and the FBI/ATF/IRS/DOJ…etc, as well as the censorship exhibited by the Democratic Party - not within the MAGA movement.

How Do You Counter This Ignorance?

In response, the education reforms proposed call for a greater emphasis on promoting free thinking and entrepreneurship through family choice. This would involve incorporating more opportunities for students to engage in entrepreneurship and internship programs, with the goal of cultivating a new generation of innovators and business leaders.

The underlying belief is that by fostering a stronger entrepreneurial spirit and a deeper understanding of the principles of free-market capitalism, students will be better equipped to contribute to the long-term stability and prosperity of the constitutional republic.

This, in turn, will lead to the strengthening of family structures and a more robust civil society, ultimately reinforcing American core values and institutions that are the foundation of a healthy country. New schools and institutions that develop these innovative curriculum policies with solid, motivated teachers will soon find that their institutions will flourish and be flushed with cash. These new schools will be bastions of cutting-edge learning as families will gladly put their dollars towards an innovative and moral education for their children.

The irony is that current C.F.S.M teachers and administrators will fight this to death because it disrupts their power, but in truth, it only disrupts the bottom half of teachers who are C.F.S.M and are terrible at their craft.

Administrators who are not good teachers, to begin with, are somewhat useless in the system and need phasing out as most all are C.F.S.M and follow the money. Good teachers will follow the learning; bad teachers follow the money. Truly innovative teachers and teachers dedicated to learning will embrace all these changes because they and their students will shine for many, many years to come. The reality is that the only thing being removed from the system is **waste**, as the time on task will be equal, if not greater, and certainly more productive given all the dead time in prison schools.

As C.F.S.M fades from education and healthcare, so will hate groups like ANTIFA and others, while families will gain power and take their rightful place at the heart of our American Constitutional Republic.

Chapter 4: True Freedom of the Press: Can It Ever Happen?

In the annals of human history, few ideals have been as cherished and simultaneously as elusive as true freedom of the press. This concept, enshrined in the First Amendment of the United States Constitution, stands as a testament to the foresight of our founding fathers. Yet, as we navigate the complexities of the 21st century, we are compelled to ask: Did we ever truly have freedom of the press, and will we ever see it again? What does this mean for families?

The Foundation of Freedom

To understand the significance of press freedom, we must first examine its roots in the very foundation of our nation. The First Amendment, which guarantees freedom of speech, press, religion, assembly, and the right to petition the government, is not merely the First Amendment by chance. It is the cornerstone upon which the entire edifice of American democracy and our republic rests. Without these fundamental freedoms, the United States would cease to exist, and it seems to be on that path.

The framers of the Constitution understood that a free and independent press was essential to the functioning of a healthy and informed constitutional republic. They recognized that an informed population was crucial for holding those in power accountable and making sound decisions in the governance of the nation. As Thomas

Jefferson famously said, "Were it left to me to decide whether we should have a government without newspapers, or newspapers without a government, I should not hesitate a moment to prefer the latter."

The Challenge of the Information Age

However, the rapid pace of technological advancement and the explosion of information in our modern society have posed unprecedented challenges to the ideal of press freedom. Governments, often struggling to keep up with these changes, have resorted to suppressing information to maintain control and true tyranny. This suppression, ironically, moves us further away from the principles of a constitutional republic, where representatives are meant to reflect the will of an informed populace.

The danger in this shift is that it pushes us toward a system ruled by the masses, who are highly susceptible to manipulation and misinformation. This is precisely why authoritarian regimes often co-opt the term "democracy" to their advantage by conflating the emotion of mobs with the democratic majority. By controlling the flow of information through propaganda and repression, they can effectively control the people while maintaining a facade of popular rule. This is why we have a **"constitutional republic"** vs. a straight **"democracy."** It is to reason out positions and then elect a representative to vote on their behalf in a reasoned manner. It is also responsible for the "electoral college" vs. straight popular vote… same principle.

The Importance of Truth – Should Be Self-explanatory...

In this context, the importance of truth becomes paramount. **A constitutional republic relies on the truth of the current and of the past as the foundation of communication between the governed and their representatives.** When the press is truly free, it serves as a conduit for accurate information, allowing citizens to make informed decisions and enabling representatives to act in accordance with the genuine will of their constituents.

However, when press freedom is compromised, the entire system begins to break down. Distorted information leads to misinformed citizens, which in turn results in ineffective or emotionalized representation. This creates a vicious cycle where the interests of the powerful are prioritized over those of the general public, further eroding the principles of democratic republic governance.

The Threat to the First Amendment

It is no coincidence that any tyrant seeking to undermine a constitutional republic would start by targeting the First Amendment. The suppression of free speech and press inevitably leads to the suppression of the electorate and, ultimately, to control of the narrative. This process is not always overt; in fact, in modern times, it often occurs through more subtle means and nefarious people. We are witnessing this phenomenon unfold before our eyes through the coordinated efforts of social media networks and the growing corporate control of media outlets. The consolidation of media ownership into the hands of a few powerful corporations poses a significant threat to the free flow of information.

When companies like Amazon own major news outlets like the Washington Post or when media conglomerates like Comcast control networks such as NBC, Paramount owning CBS, Warner Bros. owning CNN, and Disney owning ABC, the potential for conflicts of interest and biased reporting becomes alarmingly high.

When you combine this with the influence of TikTok, Instagram, Snapchat…etc., and the willingness of their CEOs to cooperate with the government, as evidenced during COVID and other instances of suppression, it resembles true Fascism. The blended C.F.S.M model involves blending a little of each platform at critical timing points, ensuring that a "good crisis," as Rahm Emanuel put it, never goes to waste.

The Corporate Threat to Press Freedom

Corporations, by their very nature, are not designed to prioritize the public good. Their primary objective is to generate profits for their shareholders, often at the expense of ethical considerations. This single-minded pursuit of financial gain leads to a distortion of the truth and a manipulation of public opinion to serve corporate interests. In the context of media ownership, this creates a dangerous situation where the entities responsible for informing the public are beholden to corporate agendas rather than journalistic integrity. The result is a news landscape that often prioritizes sensationalism, partisan narratives, and clickbait over factual, nuanced reporting.

The 24/7 News Cycle and Information Overload

The late, great Rush Limbaugh used to refer to the media as the "drive-by media," as they often seemed to share a singular thought. He even made numerous parody compilations highlighting this. While it was funny, it also highlighted the bias and centralized control of messaging, which is very sad.

The advent of the 24/7 news cycle has further complicated matters. In the past, news was typically confined to a few hours of nightly coverage, allowing time for fact-checking and thoughtful analysis. Today, the constant demand for content has created an environment where speed often trumps accuracy.

This relentless barrage of information, much of it distorted or outright false, has made it increasingly difficult for the average citizen to discern truth from fiction as organizations want to make money off the news and don't wish to be the odd organization out, hence the same messaging. The powers that be, including both government entities and corporate media owners, have recognized the potential of this constant news cycle to control messaging and manipulate public perception through coordinated propaganda. By flooding the information space with carefully crafted narratives, they can effectively shape the public's understanding of events and issues to suit their own agendas and then have it repeated over and over again in the "drive-by media."

The Evolution of True Power - Information

To truly understand the current state of press freedom and its implications for democracy, we must examine the nature of power itself. John Kenneth Galbraith, in his work "The Anatomy of Power," provides a valuable framework for understanding how power has evolved over time.

Galbraith identified three forms of power: condign power (force), compensatory power (wealth and influence), and conditioned power (control of information and ideas). In our modern era, it is this third form of power that has become dominant. The ability to shape public discourse through control of media channels has become the most potent tool for those seeking to wield influence over society.

This evolution of power presents a significant challenge to the ideals of press freedom and democratic republic governance. If human nature is driven by the desire for dominance and control, there will always be those who seek to manipulate information for their own gain. The task before us, then, is to find ways to counteract this tendency and preserve the integrity of our information ecosystem so that families aren't controlled. To truly change the power dynamic, we must change how the information is controlled and disseminated.

The Challenge of Truth in the Age of Misinformation

Combating the concentration of power through the pursuit of truth is an immense challenge, particularly in the face of the relentless propaganda and misinformation disseminated through various media outlets. It often feels like a lone voice shouting against a cacophony of millions, all repeating the same manufactured narratives.

The root of this problem lies in the current structure of the media industry, where corporations have gained control over the primary sources of information. When combined with the darker aspects of human nature - greed, ambition, and the desire for power - the results can be catastrophic for the free flow of information and the health of our republic. Isn't it obvious? The control is real.

Restoring Trust in Media – Can it be Done?

To address this issue, we must consider radical changes to the way our media landscape is structured. **The first step must be a complete or very solid separation of corporations from the controlling ownership and control of legitimate news and information sources**. While social media platforms can remain under corporate control, they should not be classified as credible news or information outlets but as populist wings of interest, especially since nobody can accurately reflect who is real and who is not online, and parents must have the ability to sue these social media companies more easily. Instead, we need to develop new, prime sources of information that the average person can access and trust. We must strive to recreate the environment of trust that existed during eras like that of Walter Cronkite, when people could tune in to the news, listen to trusted anchors, and feel confident in the information they had received.

I believe that we shouldn't go back to having only a few news sources. The variety of voices and perspectives enabled by modern technology is important. Nevertheless, we should figure out how to blend this diversity with a renewed focus on journalistic integrity and fact-based reporting. For instance, perhaps having three incorrect or false stories could lead to the removal of journalists, or we might also consider implementing a system to flag broadcasts that have been flagged for false stories. The point is it can be done as information is the real power and families need to wield it.

The Future Role of Social Media

Social media platforms have become a double-edged sword in the realm of information dissemination. On the one hand, they have democratized the ability to share information and ideas, giving voice to perspectives that might otherwise go unheard with tremendous speed of delivery. On the other hand, they have also become powerful tools for the spread of misinformation and the manipulation of public opinion through mob rule. The unchecked power of these platforms to arbitrarily silence or restrict voices is a grave threat to freedom of speech and press. These companies must be held accountable through legal means, with the ability to be sued for their actions when they overstep the bounds of reasonable content moderation. That fear of being held financially accountable alone will correct much of the tyrannical behavior.

However, simply reining in social media companies is not enough. We must also address the broader challenge of restoring the public's ability to access the truth. In an ideal world, finding accurate information should be as easy as a few clicks. When individuals are constantly being redirected by Google or other platforms to misleading advertising or false information, the propaganda wins, and the foundations of our republic are eroded.

The Two-Party System and Mob Rule

The current state of our political system, with its entrenched two-party divide, has exacerbated the problems of misinformation and manipulation. Both sides of the political spectrum have shown a tendency towards mob mentality, driven more by partisan loyalty than by a genuine concern for the greater good. This divide is the exact fear expressed by the founding fathers. They all wanted to avoid the civil wars that ripped England apart and Hamilton, Washington, Madison were all against it but Jefferson was for them… eventually Jefferson's thoughts won out and the divisions began. If the current parties began all debates and commercials with exactly where they stood on the top 10 issues, then the public would be so much better informed.

While large political rallies, whether for Trump or any other candidate, may generate excitement, they also carry the risk of devolving into mob rule. This is fundamentally at odds with the principles of a constitutional republic, where reasoned debate and the rule of law should prevail over emotional fervor and groupthink. However, in Trump's case, he has little choice as the C.F.S.M system is so heavily stacked against him that he must resort to rallies to get his message heard.

Our elected representatives, who should be the bulwark against such tendencies, have often proven themselves unequal to the task. Many have fallen victim to the same forces of propaganda and misinformation that they purport to oppose, prioritizing party loyalty and re-election over the genuine needs and interests of their constituents, which is why we need new criteria to run for office…more to follow.

A Path Forward for All

Addressing these complex and interrelated issues will require a multi-faceted approach. First and foremost, we must work towards the **elimination of corporate ownership of media** outlets. This could be replaced with a model that draws funding from a combination of private entities, stock plans with limited ownership and public ownership sources, similar to the structure of public broadcasting but with stronger safeguards against government C.F.S.M influence by putting more of the public on boards with increased transparency. Simultaneously, we need to implement stronger regulations on social media platforms, **holding them accountable** for their role in the spread of misinformation while also protecting freedom of speech in addition to protecting children. This could involve treating these platforms more like public utilities, with clear privatization guidelines for content moderation and avenues for appeal when content is removed or accounts are suspended.

Education must also play a crucial role in our efforts to restore the integrity of our information ecosystem through massive internship programs. We need to prioritize media literacy and critical thinking skills in our educational curriculum, equipping future generations with the tools they need to navigate the complex media landscape and discern truth from fiction. Furthermore, we must work to restore a sense of civic duty and engagement among the public. This involves not only encouraging participation in the political process but also fostering a culture of respectful dialogue and debate. We need to move away from the current climate of partisan hostility and towards a more constructive approach to addressing our differences.

The Role of Individual Responsibility

While systemic changes are crucial, we must also recognize the role that each of us plays as individuals in shaping our information environment. It is incumbent upon each **citizen** to take responsibility for seeking out the truth to the best of their abilities rather than passively consuming whatever information is presented to them. This means actively seeking out diverse sources of information, fact-checking claims before sharing them, and being willing to engage in respectful dialogue with those who hold different views. It also means being willing to admit when we are wrong and to change our minds in the face of new evidence.

Moreover, we must become more actively involved in the process of change at the local level. This could involve attending town hall meetings, getting on school boards, participating in local elections, or even running for office ourselves. By engaging directly with the political process, we can help to ensure that our representatives are truly accountable to the people they serve.

The Future of Press Freedom and Constitutional Republic

The challenges facing press freedom and, by extension, our constitutional republic system are formidable. The forces of power and corruption have entrenched themselves deeply within the fabric of our society, and reversing this trend will require sustained effort and commitment.

However, we must not lose sight of the immense importance of this struggle. The future of our constitutional republic and the well-being of our nation depends upon our ability to restore integrity to our media landscape and to rekindle the spirit of informed civic engagement that has been the hallmark of our American constitutional republic at its best. As we move forward, we must keep in mind the words of Supreme Court Justice Anthony Kennedy, who warned that "the First Amendment's freedoms are most vulnerable when the government seeks to control thought or to justify its laws for that impermissible end. Our right to think freely, to express ourselves without fear of reprisal, and to access accurate information is the bedrock upon which all our other freedoms rest."

The path ahead will not be easy, but it is one that we must traverse if we are to preserve the principles of freedom, equality, and justice that have long been the aspirational core of the American experiment. By working together, putting families first, staying vigilant, and never losing sight of the fundamental importance of truth and press freedom, we can hope to overcome the divisive forces that threaten to tear our society apart and forge a path toward a more informed, engaged, and truly independent future.

In this endeavor, we must draw inspiration from the courage and foresight of our founding fathers, who recognized the critical importance of a free press in maintaining a healthy constitutional republic. We must honor their legacy by rising to the challenges of our time, adapting their principles to the realities of the modern world while never losing sight of the fundamental truths they enshrined in our Constitution.

The struggle for true freedom of the press is, in essence, a struggle for the soul of our constitutional republic. It is a battle that must be fought not just in the halls of power or in the boardrooms of media conglomerates but in the hearts and minds of every citizen who values truth, justice, and the principles of democratic governance. As we face this challenge, let us remember that the power to shape our future lies not just in the hands of the few but in the collective will and actions of the many. The future of press freedom, and indeed of our constitutional republic itself, rests in our hands.

Chapter 5: Stop the Bleeding: Immigration, Judges, Crime and Honest Elections

As we look around at the current state of our nation, it's clear we are facing a crisis of trust. The speed of media, the breakdown of faith in our institutions, and the growing divides among citizens have all contributed to a deeply cynical and distrustful atmosphere. Overcoming this will require a concerted, multi-pronged effort to address the core challenges we face.

In this chapter, we will explore three critical areas that must be addressed to restore trust in America: **immigration and citizenship, crime and the justice system, and election integrity**. By tackling these issues head-on with bold, principled solutions, we can begin to heal the rifts in our society and recapture the unity of purpose that has defined our nation throughout history.

Illegal Immigration and Erosion of Citizenship

At the heart of the trust crisis is the issue of massive illegal immigration and the corresponding devaluing of American citizenship. The United States has long been a beacon of hope for those seeking a better life, earning the moniker of the "great melting pot." But the current scale and nature of illegal immigration threatens to undermine the very foundations of that proud legacy echoed by the Statue of

Liberty. We are a nation of laws, and as such, the law must be upheld. It's no secret that one political party has aggressively pushed for dramatically increased immigration, both legal and, more importantly, illegal, in recent years. The motives behind this push are not altruistic. By flooding the country with large numbers of illegal immigrants, often with the promise of future voting rights and benefits, the goal seems to be destabilizing the existing political and social order in a variety of ways.

The theory, if you can call it that, is that by diluting the citizen base, you can erode the strength of America's constitutional republic and move toward a system of "mob rule" that can be more easily controlled by the C.F.S.M communist. And when you combine this with the ability to manipulate social media and public narratives, the path to power for those with authoritarian tendencies becomes clear.

Make no mistake - what we are witnessing is tantamount to an invasion, not simply a humanitarian effort to provide refuge. The sheer scale of illegal immigration in recent years, with over 9 million (nobody knows for sure) crossing the border under the current administration, is overwhelming communities and straining resources across the country. And the unsavory elements that piggyback on this influx, from human traffickers to drug cartels, are causing immense harm as crimes are dramatically up and only getting worse.

The massive proliferation of fentanyl coming across the border is nothing short of a full declaration of war against whoever is supplying it. According to Statista 2024, the number of overdose deaths from fentanyl rose from a mere 730 in 1999 to over 73,800 in 2022, and it continues to rise, and all is correlated to the massive increase in illegal immigration.

The sex trade preying on vulnerable illegal immigrants, including children, is a particularly heinous byproduct of this crisis. It's a modern-day slave trade, repackaged to evade detection. The sad truth is that far too many of our leaders seem willing to turn a blind eye to this atrocity in pursuit of their C.F.S.M political objectives. This willful ignorance demonstrated by multiple politicians, including the president and vice president, is tantamount to a crime.

So, how do we stop this dangerous trend and restore the value of American citizenship? It starts with **securing the border** and regaining control of our immigration system. The previous administration made progress on this front with the border wall project, but much work remains. We need a comprehensive strategy that combines physical barriers, advanced surveillance, and a crackdown on employers who knowingly hire illegal workers and much more.

Again, a demonstrated willful ignorance of the value of protecting a border is somewhat frightening. Numerous civilizations have erected walls to protect themselves, as evidenced by the Great Wall in China, which was built over a period of more than 2000 years from the 7th century BCE to the 16th century CE. It was built by 19 different dynasties with the intent of protecting the northern border, preserving the Chinese culture, protecting the Silk Road trade, and creating a degree of comfort for the southern civilizations as they felt secure. What we are doing is no different than what China did when it built its Great Wall to protect itself.

At the same time, we must address the incentives that draw migrants to enter the country illegally. Eliminating "anchor baby" citizenship completely and imposing significant fines or back taxes on those who have broken the law are crucial steps along with the mass deportation of illegals. Curbing the ability of criminal enterprises to profit from human trafficking and the drug trade is also essential and a clear, immediate military objective.

But it's not enough to simply restrict and punish. We must also create clearer, more accessible pathways to **legal** immigration and citizenship for those who wish to contribute to our society through their skills and talents. By welcoming the "best and brightest" from around the world, we can harness the energy and innovation that has fueled American exceptionalism throughout our history. We have many of these policies in place and only need to tweak them. The key is to enforce these policies as we are a nation of laws.

Protecting citizens is the primary function of any United States President, and there should be a special process for impeaching a president who fails to protect citizens from foreign invasions, which is what 9 to 20 million (no exact number) illegal immigrants are tantamount to.

The key is finding the right balance – and while doing so, securing our borders, upholding the existing rule of law, and yet remaining true to our identity as a nation of immigrants. It's a delicate dance, but one that is vital to restoring faith in the value of American citizenship. When everyone has a stake in the system and the rules apply equally to all, then we can start to rebuild the trust that has been so badly eroded.

When it becomes evident that illegal immigrants can cross the border and access resources intended for citizens, this situation will persist until it is addressed. Not only must it be stopped, but it should also be penalized and discouraged to prevent recurring issues. The families of the United States are the ones who suffer the most from this.

The strain on government resources is overwhelming and is already straining the system. The welfare, education, and housing systems are all under pressure, while hardworking families bear the burden. Every parent reading this should demand expenditure numbers for illegal immigrant services from their C.F.S.M school and this will all begin to make sense.

For the American people to truly grasp the financial and social impact of illegal immigration on government resources, a **detailed line-item budget** should be created that accounts for all associated costs. This budget should be transparently shared with society. Only then will people recognize the significant financial toll of these policies when they see the thousands of dollars collected by the IRS as part of this system. Each and every time you hear the words **"continuing resolution,"** you should get upset. Continuing resolutions are at the heart of the problem because they continue to lump in all money to fund all of government and all of government programs, including all of this illegal immigration.

The **"smoke and mirrors"** argument that we hear all the time is that "we have to pay our bills," which of course we do, but the argument is false in that we have enough money to pay all our bills with tax receipts, if we simply stop spending excessively on the things American people don't want, and one of them is illegal immigration. If every citizen were presented with an annual bill through the IRS for illegal immigration, you'd see how fast funding would stop, but we will never know because of the continuing resolutions.

So, by getting back to passing regular order budgets, the American people will see exactly how much it costs each of us to continue these programs, and when we are taxed accordingly to fund this, there aren't many rational people who would say yes. But, all of this is hidden from the American public in **continuing resolutions**.

When those most affected—typically lower-income families—are faced with an annual bill in addition to job loss to sustain illegal immigration, public sentiment will likely shift dramatically against this issue.

Crime, Judges, and the Assault on Justice

Closely linked to the illegal immigration crisis is the alarming rise in crime that has afflicted many of our communities courtesy of the design by the C.F.S.M communists. As waves of unvetted illegal immigrants have flooded across the border, often with no means of support, the temptation to turn to illicit activities has proved irresistible for far too many. Gangs, drug trafficking, sex slave trade and violent offenses have all spiked to disturbing levels, and it is affecting us all.

And just as troubling is the response, or lack thereof, from our justice system. Instead of holding criminals accountable, we've seen a disturbing trend of "activist" judges and C.F.S.M communists who seem more interested in advancing a political agenda than upholding the law. These magistrates, many of whom have been appointed by politicians beholden to radical ideologies, have routinely handed down lenient sentences, allowed dangerous suspects back onto the streets without bail money, and even refused to prosecute certain categories of crimes altogether.

It's a recipe for societal breakdown, as law-abiding citizens find themselves living in fear, unable to trust the very institutions meant to protect them. Families are forced into "helicopter parenting," terrified to let their children venture outside in some cases. Businesses struggle to operate in an environment of constant uncertainty, lawlessness and threat. And the fabric of the community, that essential glue that holds a civilization together, begins to fray, as does the family unit.

The root of this crisis lies in a dangerous convergence of interests. On one side, you have the criminal cartel element - the gangs, the traffickers, the predators - who recognize that our weakened justice system represents their best opportunity to operate with impunity. On the other hand, there is a cadre of ideologically driven judges and prosecutors who see this breakdown as a means to an end with money as a motivator, all so they can get a better seat at the C.F.S.M communist table.

These activist magistrates are not interested in the impartial application of the law. Their goal is to advance a radical, anti-American agenda under the guise of "criminal justice reform." By undermining the ability of law enforcement to maintain order and by subverting the integrity of the judicial process, they hope to sow chaos and erode public confidence in the very institutions that stand as bulwarks against tyranny.

It's a twisted and malevolent game, one that plays out against the backdrop of a larger struggle for power against American families. You see, the true communist elite - the billionaires and political kingpins who bankroll this agenda - recognize that a society in turmoil is ripe for their taking. By creating a **power vacuum** at the local level, they can swoop in and fill it with a federal police force that answers to them alone. So historically reminiscent of the days of Hitler's Gestapo.

The "defund the police" movement has played right into this sinister plot by design. The true C.F.S.M communist never lets a racial crisis or any crisis go to waste. This is exactly how the defunding of the police movement started (Thank you, Barack Obama, for stoking the seeds of hatred).

By starving municipal law enforcement of resources and branding them as racist oppressors, the stage has been set for a federal takeover. And let's be clear - the FBI, the IRS, the ATF, and the Department of Justice (DOJ) under the current administration are more than happy to seize this opportunity, no matter the cost to individual liberty and community safety. These once-revered institutions have now become tools for the communist elite to manipulate, as they control the leadership of all the organizations.

The sheer power wielded by these institutions paralyzes even the most honest government employees, preventing them from doing the right thing for fear of financial ruin.

So, how do we fight back against this assault on justice? The first step is to address the rot at the core of the judicial system itself. We must implement a mechanism to swiftly remove activist judges who routinely issue rulings that violate the Constitution. A simple formula like five or ten overturned cases on constitutional grounds, and you're out for a year, with the possibility of a probationary return. Those who cannot uphold their solemn oath to defend the founding document have no business sitting on the bench. After their return, if they have one more case overturned on constitutional grounds, they are permanently out.

At the same time, we need to purge the ranks of rogue prosecutors - the Attorney Generals who have weaponized their offices against the very citizens they are sworn to protect. These individuals, many of whom have risen to power through the sponsorship of radical special interests, must be held accountable for their abuses of power. Targeting law-abiding citizens under the guise of "lawfare" cannot be tolerated.

But it's not enough to simply remove the bad actors. We must also restore the proper balance of discretion and consequences within the justice system. Judges should have the latitude to consider extenuating circumstances and apply appropriate leniency in sentencing in accordance with constitutional law. However, that discretion cannot extend to a de facto elimination of punishment for repeat offenders or violent criminals.

Bail reform has become a troubling buzzword in recent years, with some jurisdictions effectively eliminating cash bail altogether. This is an insanely dangerous development that removes a crucial deterrent to criminal behavior. There must be consequences, real consequences, for those who choose to prey upon the innocent. And the scales of justice must be weighted in favor of public safety, not the whims of ideologues.

UPHOLDING THE 2nd AMENDMENT

Lastly, we must vigilantly and vigorously defend the Second Amendment rights of law-abiding citizens. The right to bear arms is the ultimate safeguard against **tyranny**, as the Japanese high command recognized during World War II when they opted not to invade the mainland United States. An armed populace is a deterrent to those who would seek to subjugate us, whether they be **foreign invaders or**

domestic authoritarians. Make no mistake - the assault on the Second Amendment, like the defunding of police, is **part of a broader strategy to disarm the citizenry and consolidate power at the federal level**. Those who seek to strip us of this fundamental freedom are the true enemies of constitutional republics, no matter how they cloak their intentions in the language of "public safety."

Ask yourself a simple question: which governments throughout history have attempted to disarm their people and why? The most notable governments that come to mind are, of course, Nazi Germany, the Cambodian regime under Pol Pot, and the Soviet Union under Stalin. Do these sound like altruistic, freedom-loving governments? Do you think they put the family first?

The Second Amendment must **never** be removed. No lists detailing who owns guns and who doesn't should ever exist because it's the first step to disarming the public. And never forget the most basic of all, which is that to stop a bad guy or a lunatic with a gun, you need a good person with a gun to stop them. The key to resolution on this isn't to take or remove guns from law-abiding citizens; the key is to punish criminals that use guns nefariously and unjustly.

There is so much more that can be said about this, but the main point is that we need to stop demonizing law-abiding gun owners. It is our right to bear arms, and even George Washington himself strongly advocated for this right. The truth is, there is nothing in this amendment that prohibits us from owning military weapons of equal grade to that of our military. However, the C.F.S.M. communists want to take away even handguns. This right should NEVER be taken away. Peace through strength extends to us all first, the world second!

By restoring integrity to our justice system, holding criminals accountable, and safeguarding the rights of law-abiding Americans, we can begin to rebuild the trust that has been so badly eroded. A populace that feels secure in their persons and property and believes the scales of justice will be balanced fairly is far less likely to succumb to the siren song of authoritarianism.

Election Integrity: The Linchpin of Trust

At the heart of a functioning constitutional republic lies the sacred right of the people to choose their representatives. Yet, in recent years, we have witnessed a steady erosion of the integrity and transparency that should define our electoral processes. From the troubling anomalies of the 2020 election to the ongoing efforts to undermine basic safeguards, the very foundations of our democratic system are being called into question.

It's a dangerous situation, for without faith in the fairness and legitimacy of our elections, the social contract that binds us together as a nation begins to unravel. After all, what good is the right to vote if the system is rigged and if the will of the people can be subverted by shadowy forces with a political agenda?

When we combine these coordinated efforts with the amount of misinformation that has been spread by various news and social media outlets, it becomes extremely difficult for any family to make **well-informed decisions**. They are constantly battling marketing tactics and misinformation. This goes against the intentions of our founding fathers and every soldier who gave his life for this right above all else.

This past election is not merely a theoretical concern. The 2020 election, with its deluge of mail-in ballots, unmonitored drop boxes, and questionable vote-counting procedures, raised serious red flags for anyone concerned with preserving the integrity of our republic. Documentaries like "2,000 Mules" have shone a light on troubling irregularities, from the mysteriously pristine, unfolded mail-in ballots to the suspicious movements of ballot traffickers in key swing states via cell phone tracking data.

The simple fact is that in a system where the electoral college, not the popular vote, determines the outcome, small shifts in a handful of counties can make all the difference in a tight race. And when you combine all the various anomalies that were observed, from the late-night ballot dumps to the questionable disqualification of legitimate poll watchers, the picture that emerges is one of a concerted effort to tip the scales. Whether those efforts ultimately succeeded in swinging the final result is a matter of debate. The Department of Justice, in its current incarnation, has shown no inclination to pursue any meaningful investigation, which is odd on its face. But the damage to public trust has been done, and it is incumbent upon us to implement reforms that will restore faith in the sanctity of the vote. Time to move forward.

It's still mind-boggling to just about every American how a 50-year entrenched career politician with multiple failed presidential runs, Joe Biden, received far more votes than the popular Barack Obama and Trump, two very public presidents. However, that's water under the bridge, and it is time to move on since the damage has been done.

The solution, in my view, is deceptively simple - create a national multiday holiday for federal elections, as Sean Hannity would say, to be held over the course of two, even three full days.

A full shutdown of everything to accommodate all voting, no excuses. No more early voting, no more drop boxes, and certainly no more of the chaotic, protracted vote-counting processes that have become all too common. Just two/three days, one federal holiday, where every eligible citizen can cast their ballot with the full confidence that their voice is being heard.

Pair this with a requirement for photo ID and possibly fingerprint verification on all absentee ballots tied to citizens, and you've taken a major step toward securing the integrity of the system. After all, we demand photo ID for everything from air travel to basic financial and welfare transactions. The notion that this is somehow "discriminatory" is simply absurd. Currently, possession of a valid ID is a baseline requirement for full civic participation. Why not use it?

And let's not forget the importance of poll watchers and observers from both parties who can monitor the entire process and ensure transparency with 3rd party vote counting. The arbitrary disqualification of legitimate poll watchers in 2020, often on dubious grounds, was a clear indication of the communist C.F.S.M forces at work to undermine faith in the system.

Term Qualifications Not Term Limits

However, securing the voting process is only half the battle. We must also look at the qualifications and character of those who seek elected office. Too often, we've seen lawyers and career politicians rise to positions of power, individuals more concerned with advancing a partisan agenda than serving the best interests of the nation.

The corruption in the system can directly be attributed to long-serving, power-hungry, money-seeking career politicians who have been in power for 40-50 years. This type of politician must end for all our sakes.

A mandatory requirement of **ten years of private sector experience** before any individual can run for public office should be the norm. No more ivory tower dwellers, no more career bureaucrats. We need people who have lived and worked in the real world and who understand the challenges facing everyday Americans. And term limits, or perhaps better termed "term qualifications," should be established to prevent the calcification of the political class. Robust candidate debates, held at schools, in parks, and on prime-time television and moderated by respected non-partisan figures like parents, should also be a cornerstone of the electoral process and much more common. The American people deserve to hear directly from those who seek to lead them and scrutinize their policies and vision in a public forum, not in a bombardment of highly slanted TV ads. No more canned, scripted performances - give us genuine discourse and the clash of ideas.

Taken together, these reforms - a national holiday for voting, secure ballot procedures, qualified candidates, and transparent debates - represent a blueprint for restoring trust in the democratic process. When the citizens of this great nation can be confident that their votes carry weight and that the system is not rigged against them, then we will have taken a giant leap toward healing the divisions that have threatened to tear us apart.

And make no mistake - this is not a partisan issue. True patriots, regardless of political affiliation, should recognize the vital importance of safeguarding the integrity of our elections. If we allow the forces of corruption and authoritarianism to erode that foundation, then the entire edifice of our constitutional republic will crumble.

The Path Forward

Taken together, the pillars we've explored – ending illegal immigration and improving the value of citizenship, punishing crime, politician qualifications, the justice system accountability, and true election integrity - represent the cornerstones of restoring trust in America and will go a long way toward establishing stronger trusting families and better communities.

By addressing these fundamental challenges with clarity, conviction, and a steadfast commitment to our founding principles, we can begin to rebuild the bonds that have sustained us through times of crisis and turmoil.

It will not be an easy task. The forces arrayed against us - the ideologues, the power-hungry, the corrupters of our civic institutions - will fight tooth and nail to maintain their grip on the levers of control. But we must not shrink from this fight, for the stakes are too high. The very future of our nation, our way of life, hangs in the balance.

It is a daunting task, to be sure. But we are a resilient and resolute people, forged in the crucible of adversity time and time again. We have overcome great challenges before, and we will do so again. For in the end, the principles that define us - liberty, justice, dignity and opportunity - are more powerful than any forces that seek to undermine them.

So, let us roll up our sleeves and get to work. Let us reclaim our birthright as citizens of the greatest nation on earth, a beacon of hope to all who yearn to breathe free air.

And let us show the world that the spirit of America, the unbreakable will of a free people, can never be extinguished or subjugated.

Chapter 6: Capitalism: Time to Unleash Its True Power

The current state of economic understanding among politicians and the public is alarmingly low. Too many of our elected leaders display a complete lack of knowledge when it comes to the fundamentals of economic policies and how our economy truly functions. This lack of understanding is echoed in our education system, where comprehensive economic education is often neglected until the senior year of high school, if at all. This profound dearth of understanding impacts families, directly and indirectly, and must be corrected if we are ever to have experienced private sector politicians from a new generation.

Recently, we witnessed this firsthand when Vice President Kamala Harris was asked about the economy and her policy proposals. Her immediate response was to blame "price gouging by food companies" as a solution to the problem of inflation. This approach is horribly misguided and dangerous, and it has been repeatedly tried throughout history with disastrous consequences. It is known by serious people to be flawed. When you combine this lack of basic understanding with a tendency to distort history, you are setting the stage for human suffering, as America will fall. If America falls, the world will fall.

In the 1930s, Joseph Stalin's attempts to control the means of production through his five-year plan resulted in the deaths of nearly 11 million Ukrainians. Similarly, Mao

Zedong's policies in China to control the economy led to the deaths of over 25 million people. These examples demonstrate the **negative externalities** and **market distortions** that occur when governments intervene in the **free market** system.

Our capitalist system, with all its flaws, has been the primary driver of economic growth and prosperity in the United States, lifting the standard of living for millions of citizens and contributing to the betterment of lives around the world through our charitable programs and economic initiatives. Yet, we are now again facing a worrying rise in the tide of the C.F.S.M communist, which threatens to undermine the very foundations of our economic system.

The Capitalist System is The Best Economic System Ever Created

At the core of our American economic success is the **capitalist system**, which is based on the fundamental principles of freedom, **choice and scarcity of goods**. Simply put, individuals and businesses have the **freedom to choose** what to produce, what to consume, and how to allocate their **resources** through **supply and demand,** with **pricing** at its core. This freedom of choice is the driving force behind innovation, risk-taking, and the **efficient allocation of resources.**

The founding of our nation in 1776 coincided with the publication of Adam Smith's seminal work, "The Wealth of Nations," which laid the groundwork for the principles of capitalism. Smith's treatise on the growth of wealth and the true measure of a country's prosperity has stood the test of time despite its complexity and the challenges of making its lessons accessible to the general public. Only the actual American Revolution in 1776, depicted on the cover, could actually surpass the long-standing importance of Smith's work, and the two linked together have defined America.

One of the key tenets of capitalism is the idea that individuals who contribute bring **efficiency** to the system. However, there is an evil concept known as the "**free rider**" problem, which is a natural outgrowth of the human condition, and it comes from massive exposure to socialist and communist systems, where individuals are incentivized to **consume** more than they **produce** in many cases without even realizing it and without contributing at all.

As former President John F. Kennedy eloquently stated, "Ask not what your country can do for you, but what you can do for your country." This call to action is a direct challenge to the **free rider** mentality and a recognition of the importance of individual contribution to the greater good.

This is not about contributing on behalf of the state but about contributing to the economy by creating and competing for yourself and improving your standard of living and that of your family. By doing this, you will not depend on the government, and you will contribute to the greater good by allowing the government to focus on those who are less fortunate. Free riders create massive dissension among us all, as their actions go against the very concept of fairness and the constant focus on "victimization" has made it worse. While there will always be individuals who require more assistance than others due to factors like disability, lack of knowledge, or unfamiliarity with the system, these individuals should not be labeled as free riders but people in need of true assistance.

The Social Security system began during the Great Depression in 1935 under Roosevelt. It was established to support the most vulnerable members of our society, like the elderly and the impoverished. It is essential and should continue, BUT it does create free riders as its disability provisions are being abused. However, it requires a significant overhaul, a topic for another book.

Capitalism does lift all boats in a rising tide mentality, but it does have negative side effects. Not all boats are the same in this analogy, which is why this social safety net was created.

To begin, the penalties for stealing from Social Security and the safety net should be severe, as these actions trigger a cascade of negative consequences that are often irreparable.

Those genuinely in need should receive assistance, but as Jesus profoundly said, "Give a man a fish, and you feed him for a day. Teach a man to fish, and you feed him for a lifetime." This adage has stood the test of time for all cultures and is paramount to stopping "free riders" taking from the needy. The free rider problem has become increasingly pervasive with the proliferation of government spending programs, starting with the well-intentioned creation of Social Security and now stemming from Lyndon Johnson's "Great Society's" continual evolution of handing out "free" benefits for decades. This created a situation where many lack the incentive and skills to become productive members of society. This is the heart of the problem, as it destroys work ethic, creates sloths and, most importantly, crowds out public investment that could help create opportunities for new family businesses.

Current C.F.S.M communist-socialist policies, focused on providing basic necessities to keep the lowest members of society dependent, are at the root of the free rider and illegal immigration dilemmas. This approach fosters complacency and undermines the principles crucial to a thriving capitalist society.

The deleterious effect of this distorted "Santa Claus" system is felt by hard-working families who now must have both parents working to support and feed their children as the giveaways go to many non-deserving free riders. These families see the negative consequences of such policies and become discouraged, which in turn has negative effects on the rearing of their children.

It's a constant barrage of watching others feed or "free ride" off the system, which discourages honesty and hard work and leads to anxious decisions from a family perspective. Meaningful reform is necessary to restore fairness and personal accountability and to ensure that all members of society can thrive and work.

Economic Education at All Levels

To address the lack of economic understanding among the populace, it is essential to reform our education system as outlined previously. Economic education should be a core component of the curriculum from the earliest grades, ensuring that children and families are exposed to the fundamental concepts of capitalism, the role of markets, and the mechanics of the free enterprise system.

We can recall that the career options presented to students in younger grades were often limited to traditional civic roles such as firefighting, police officer, or even nursing. The teaching materials, such as puppets or other visual aids, tended to depict these conventional occupations. Very little, if any, emphasis is placed on entrepreneurship, as most teachers appear to have a limited understanding of this career path, which is ironic because it is the taxes generated by capitalism that fund all their salaries. This problem of not exposing students to entrepreneurship early persists and has become increasingly more widespread over time. Why sacrifice to create something when you can get the benefits for free?

The current state of economic education is woefully inadequate, with most students not receiving a comprehensive understanding of these critical topics until their senior year of high school, if at all. This is a disservice to our nation's youth, who are being trained as young bureaucrats, activists, or socialists rather than being encouraged to become entrepreneurs and contributors to the economic fabric of our society. In truth, every new school with academically liberated teachers should have multiple and varied courses on the evils that communism, Marxism, socialism, and fascism all presented to the planet over the last 100+ years. These failed systems need to be shown as the consummate failures they all are.

The impact on families can be devastating when children are not adequately prepared to thrive in society. Even worse, they may be encouraged to resist or rail against societal and family norms before they even understand the norms, which destabilize the family and country.

The saying by Peter Ustinov: 'Parents are the bones on which children sharpen their teeth, seems to apply at a younger age nowadays. Children who are naturally defiant receive marching instructions from the school and evil social media both directly and indirectly on how to dismiss their parents in order to become an accepted part of the current C.F.S.M communist educational system. It is destructive, which is exactly why parents must have a choice.

Parenting is very hard, and many parents are often unsure of the best path forward after high school and tend to follow the herd, so they push their children into an overpriced college environment that may continue the C.F.S.M communist activist education, where in many cases, a vocational or trade school program could be a better fit for the child and family. Our higher education system is now rife with C.F.S.M communists due to all the federal exposure to the system…This all must change, and it starts with dramatic decreases in federal support dollars that drive up costs and salaries. Similarly, many MBA (Master of Business Arts) programs place great emphasis on entrepreneurship, with the assumption that starting one's own business is universally preferable to working for an employer, which truly is great. However, this overlooks the significant challenges to get to the traditional MBA educational path - 12 years of schooling, 4 years of college, then an MBA - often produces "professional students" who lack practical experience and the necessary skills to achieve financial independence through entrepreneurship alone as they are typically very deep in educational debt. Real-world, hands-on learning and skill development may be a more effective pathway to economic success for many individuals, but the principles learned in an MBA program should be accessible to them much earlier, as it will improve their chances of business success.

The introduction of economic concepts and the principles of capitalism should begin at the pre-kindergarten level with something as simple as the game of Monopoly and continue through the entire educational journey and, more importantly, involve families every step of the way.

By the time students graduate from high school, they should possess a deep understanding coupled with solid experience of how our economic system works and, more importantly, should have enough work experience to open their own business or two, which broadens their choices and purpose. The role of government in economic policy should

UNITED STATES 12.0 – FREEDOM VS. COMMUNISM

be to facilitate this learning, not delay it, but that isn't likely with the current level of C.F.S.M communist bureaucrats we have in place who all subscribe to the academic credentialed career path, as it keeps students exposed to C.F.S.M much longer. The importance of individual initiative and risk-taking should be emphasized from day 1 of education, with economics at the core. Students and families should be able to profit while in school just as college athletes can now profit from sports and any ventures that are undertaken. The possibilities are endless.

Furthermore, the availability of economic courses and programs at the college level should be expanded, with the MBA degree potentially becoming a standard achievement by the time students complete their high school education. This would not only better prepare our youth for the realities of the business world but also foster a culture of entrepreneurship and self-reliance. Why wait to teach the principles of an MBA until after college? Of course, some financial concepts, formulas, and theories are more challenging; however, learning them in context from examples and work will greatly simplify the process. In the end, nothing bad comes from hard work, and if your family is successful, they will all work harder and create generational wealth.

One of the most inspiring examples of the power of entrepreneurship is the success of legal immigrant entrepreneurs in the United States. Time and time again, we have witnessed immigrants who are willing to work tirelessly, often putting in 50, 60, 70 or even 80 hours a week, surpassing the economic achievements of their native-born counterparts. This phenomenon is often met with envy and resentment rather than admiration and emulation. Coveting your neighbor's goods is never a good thing, as evidenced by being one of the 10 commandments, although we think coveting and emulating your neighbor's work ethic **is** a good thing.

By enhancing economic education and promoting a culture of entrepreneurship, we can empower our citizens and families to become active contributors to the system rather than passive consumers or free riders who drain the coffers of the system. This is a crucial step in strengthening the foundations of our capitalist society and family, ensuring its continued prosperity. The United States needs to expand and grow the pie not divide the pie.

To effectively navigate the complexities of our economic system, it is essential for individuals and families to have a grasp of key economic concepts, like inflation and the role of supply and demand in the market.

Inflation

Inflation is a pernicious force that disproportionately harms the lower-income segments of the population. When prices rise at a rate exceeding 2% annually, as has been the case for the past several years, the impact is felt most acutely by those living paycheck to paycheck. In some cases, cost increases have reached as high as 30%, with other sectors experiencing 20% or 15% inflation. While the rate of inflation has begun to slow in recent months, the cumulative effect of these price hikes has been devastating, akin to rapid weight gain. Just as it is challenging to lose the extra pounds gained over several years, reversing the impact of high inflation on one's financial well-being is a daunting task. Inflation is deadly as it erodes purchasing power and constricts economies, causing hardship for families just as those unwanted pounds secretly add up, and then you can't reverse the gain without serious discipline.

The root cause of this wave of inflation is again multifaceted and, in this case, mostly can be traced back to the massive spending policies implemented by the current administration, coupled with restrictive changes in regulations, oil production, and supply of energy within the United States, these massive disruptions caused uncertainty in the markets continues to wreak havoc.

These actions had and have a ripple effect, spiking transportation costs and creating distortions in **supply and demand** across various industries, causing prices to rise.

Here is where it gets tricky for families as many are tied to businesses that have all been struggling EXCEPT for the so-called "Magnificent 7," which includes Apple, Microsoft, Alphabet, Amazon, NVIDIA, Tesla and Meta Platforms. All are heavily tied to our government financially and, in many cases, in a fascistic manner. Tesla is the only one that is truly not aligned with the communist train of thought, and as a result, Musk will forever be a target. These huge businesses can weather the inflation storm much better than medium or small businesses, which is why the stock market has continually risen for all the large businesses or a good portion of them, but the rest of the market is not doing well and felt by families.

When small or medium business owners are uncertain in a rising price market, they batten down the hatches and constrict, and in many cases, go out of business, which is what we are all feeling today in this dual economy. If you are in the top 7, then you are fine…are you in them, or do you buy from them?

Tools The Government Uses

A truly supportive government should seek to alleviate the pain of families first, as the family unit is a powerful force because it can implement austerity measures on a much faster scale while, conversely, taking divergent risks to help grow the economy and their own situation. To this end, the government has two primary tools at its disposal to address inflation: **monetary policy and fiscal policy**.

Monetary policy primarily refers to the manipulation of interest rates and how much actual money is circulating within the economy, which directly impacts pricing and the cost of borrowing for major purchases such as homes, vehicles, and capital investments. **Fiscal** policy, on the other hand, involves government spending and programs designed to stimulate employment and economic activity. Most people associate this with the programs that were instituted coming out of the depression from the 30s. The best way to think of this is massive public projects like dams, bridges, or roadways to help facilitate both employment and functionality, which improves the standard of living.

However, the effective use of these tools requires a deep understanding of their interconnectedness and the potential consequences of each approach. For example, raising interest rates to combat inflation can negatively impact the housing market and slow down overall economic growth. Conversely, expansionary fiscal policies can lead to increased government spending and further exacerbate inflationary pressures.

When COVID hit, the government went crazy, handing out cash left and right, flooding the economy with way too much physical money. This, of course, led to a ton of inflationary pressure, as all that extra cash chased a limited number of goods, driving prices through the roof. And to make matters worse, the Biden administration's restrictive energy policies only added fuel to the fire, making things even more painful for everyone. If you owned a large asset like a house, you had a chance to hedge a bit, but many people just took the financial hit and have not recovered, especially renters.

If Harris wins the presidency, we can expect more of the same - a never-ending cycle of redistribution, economic pain and suffering and a growing "victimization" economy. It's a true recipe for disaster, as we're already seeing the devastating effects. The economy is an unbalanced mess from a small and business perspective, and it's only going to get worse if we don't make some serious changes. Why should seven companies make up over 30% of the stock index? That is insane. They must be broken up the same as in the early 1900s with the "robber barons."

The challenge lies in striking the right balance between these two policy levers to achieve the desired outcome of **full employment** and stable economic growth without fueling excessive inflation. This delicate balance is often misunderstood by both politicians and the public, leading to suboptimal policy decisions like the EVIL "**continuing resolution**" that can have far-reaching implications for individual families and the broader economy.

From a family perspective, we have this under control, meaning we can work, get new jobs, start a new business, and spend money on goods and services. Most importantly, families can stop spending.

The same cannot be said for the government. They're addicted to spending because politicians don't want to be the adults in the room and tell "Santa Claus" to stop spending, and it's reached catastrophic levels. We're talking a whopping $35 trillion deficit (and another $7 Trillion on the Fed's balance sheet…$42T total), which is a staggering @125% of our GDP! That's like blowing 25% more than our entire paycheck every year - a recipe for disaster.

Imagine if a family sat down at the dinner table to have a serious discussion about their finances and came up with the concept of a continuing resolution. They put all their money in one account, and then their teenage son or daughter spent it all on video games instead of food and shelter. This is essentially what is happening with our government and its screwed-up spending priorities. They are not responsible for budgeting, and the "continuing resolution" MUST stop.

You'll know when we're really in trouble when a cabal of countries break off and stop using the dollar as the world's backup currency. When that happens and some predict it'll happen in the next two years on the present political course, this debt bill will be due and payable! This means every man, woman and child as of today would be responsible for over $120,000+ each. A family of 5 could owe over $600,000+.

Then, the country will begin to experience **austerity** measures that we've never seen before. Imagine this: your child is born and already owes $120,000, and it's only getting worse. But let's save that topic for another book, as it could turn around…hopefully.

Supply and Demand

The heart of our capitalist system beats to the rhythm of **supply and demand**. This powerful force dictates the prices and availability of everything we buy, from groceries to gadgets. It's a simple concept, really: when there's more of something than people want, the price drops. Think of those giant displays at the supermarket with prices slashed – that's supply outpacing demand in action. Understanding this dynamic is key for families and individuals to make smart choices about spending and investing. This dynamic is particularly evident in the case of **elastic** goods, where consumers have the flexibility to switch between different options. However, for inelastic goods, such as essential medications, the demand remains relatively constant regardless of price changes, as consumers have no choice but to continue purchasing these items. It's not just medicine that fits this bill. Essentials like electricity, water, and even a cell phone for a kid today – these are all things we consider "must-haves." No matter what the price, we're likely to keep buying them, making them inelastic.

The dance between supply and demand isn't just about setting prices; it's about guiding how our resources are used. When something is scarce, prices climb, signaling to businesses that they need to make more to meet the demand. On the flip side, when there's too much of something, prices drop, pushing companies to cut back on production or find new ways to use their resources.

These ups and downs can be tough on families, especially when companies are forced to make cuts. That's why transparency is so important – it helps us understand the market forces at play and gives families a better chance to navigate these economic tides and make better purchase decisions and not just spend, spend and spend.

This constant feedback loop of pricing between supply and demand is the most critical component of the capitalist system, **ensuring the efficient allocation of resources and driving innovation and progress**. By understanding these dynamics, politicians, individuals and families can better navigate economic decisions, anticipate market trends, and make informed choices in education, healthcare, and their own financial well-being.

Most importantly, they can improve their standard of living and set a good example for their children to pick up the torch and move forward. Earlier, we discussed how Kamala Harris wanted to institute price controls, which is why it is necessary to understand that price controls interfere with the supply and demand decisions and the choices of individuals and companies which is why it never really works.

As advocated, the family unit is the fundamental building block of a prosperous capitalist society, and its role in shaping economic outcomes cannot be overstated. If parents are allowed to take on a more prominent role in the choice of their children's education and healthcare, the overall well-being of their household will have a much better trajectory.

They must also develop a deeper understanding of economic principles and how they can positively impact their family's financial security through the creation of opportunity.

One of the key themes of this work is the idea that the parent's level of economic comprehension directly affects their ability to create a better existence for their family. When parents have a solid grasp of economic concepts, they see every day. They can make more informed decisions, anticipate the impact of policy changes, and guide their children towards becoming active contributors to the capitalist system rather than passive consumers or free riders and greatly improve their family's standard of living.

Regulation and Capitalism

At the heart of the capitalist system is the notion of **choice**. Individuals and businesses must have the freedom to choose what they produce, what they consume, and how they allocate their resources. This freedom is the driving force behind innovation, risk-taking, and the efficient distribution of goods and services. This is why inflation and excessive regulation are so bad, as they directly distort prices.

Regulation of businesses and individuals is the communist's most favorite tool to control us. Regulation of business is necessary, especially in cases of pollution, but the overutilization of regulations empowers bureaucrats and non-elected officials (which are basically synonymous) to control both individuals and corporations in ways that are beneficial to tyrannical rule and antithetical to families and the concepts of capitalism.

Regulation becomes necessary because, in many cases, individuals take advantage of certain business situations. An enhanced, empowered, moral family unit can help reduce the need for regulations.

A higher degree of morality within a family will result in the upbringing of moral, self-reliant, and confident children. By instilling the principles of capitalism with morality within the family unit at a much more comprehensive level, parents can empower their children to become self-reliant, entrepreneurial, and contributors to the economic growth of our society while at the same time counteracting the powers of the unelected bureaucrat or communist who uses regulations to control us.

This concept of moral-based self-reliance (without government overregulation getting in the way) is extremely important because it is the building block that individuals need to really feel a sense of purpose and freedom. When groups are unfairly targeted or overregulated because of the color of their skin, their political background, their ethnicity or any other discriminating factor, they lose motivation to try to succeed. This is what gave birth to the movement of DEI -diversity, equity, and inclusion, which are being used by purely C.F.S.M communists.

The idea of America is that we are a melting pot, which was mentioned previously.

However, it is a melting pot based upon merit, not based upon where you are from or what the color of your skin is, but on merit and the content of your character, as Martin Luther King once inspired. When you put the color of your skin ahead of merit, you distort the entire capitalist mechanism and create dissension amongst groups; you enhance the concept of victimization across the board.

All those things should be abandoned in favor of simple equality through opportunity with merit as its core. The communist or unelected bureaucrat will hide behind superfluous **regulations** to promote one group over another group, which will, of course, be dependent upon which group supports the tyrannical movement. It is precisely this feigned power that we must get away from in our society.

Taxes, Charity and Capitalism

Again, one of the most significant threats to the capitalist system is the "free rider" problem, where individuals consume more from the system than they contribute. This mentality is often associated with C.F.S.M communist ideologies, where the government is seen as the provider, rather than the facilitator, of economic prosperity.

Parents must instill in their children the understanding that true prosperity comes from individual contributions and the willingness to give back in the form of charity and taxes, which are both okay. However, excessive taxation (taxation without representation) leads to redistribution and contributes to the free rider problem. Therefore, just taxation for collective goods for all to benefit from is more than fine and just.

The same goes for charitable contributions, which in a moral society is truly a just cause. This concept, as eloquently expressed by President John F. Kennedy, is a fundamental tenet of a healthy capitalist society.

By fostering a culture of contribution within the family unit, parents can help their children develop a sense of civic responsibility, a stronger work ethic, and a deeper appreciation for the system that has enabled their family's prosperity. This, in turn, will strengthen the foundations of the capitalist system and ensure its continued success. While competition is a fundamental aspect of capitalism, it's crucial to operate within a moral framework. We should strive to not only compete but also support each other, ensuring that success isn't only achieved at the expense of others. This prevents a "zero-sum game" scenario where there's only one winner and one loser. Ideally, the government should play a role in fostering a balanced playing field, but unfortunately, it often overreaches, like a biased referee unfairly influencing the outcome of a game. This is akin to the principles of C.F.S.M communism, where the government exerts excessive control and selects winners and losers, and that is what we all must fight against.

Timing, Risk-Taking and Innovation

As the primary decision-makers within the family unit, parents must develop a comprehensive understanding of economic policies and their implications. From monetary policy and its effect on interest rates to fiscal policies and their impact on employment and government spending, parents must be equipped to navigate the complexities of the economic landscape.

They must be encouraged to learn with their children as they are being introduced to new topics on capitalism in schools. This team approach will enhance entrepreneurship at all levels, thus strengthening the family unit and fostering risk-taking. By staying informed and actively engaging in the political process, parents can advocate for policies that support the growth and stability of the capitalist system while also protecting the financial well-being of their families. This may involve understanding the nuances of inflation, the role of supply and demand, the delicate balance between government intervention and the free market, and choosing the right time to take the chance in business.

Ultimately, the family unit is the cornerstone of economic prosperity, and by empowering parents to become active participants in the economic system, we can cultivate a new generation of contributors and entrepreneurs who will drive the continued success of capitalism in the United States and in the global economy.

The engine of economic growth in a capitalist system is the entrepreneurial spirit – the willingness of families and individuals to take risks, innovate, and create new products and services that drive progress and improve the standard of living. This entrepreneurial drive is a crucial component of the American experience and has been a significant contributor to the country's prosperity.

The concept of **"creative destruction."** As new technologies and business models emerge, they often disrupt existing industries and replace them with more efficient and innovative solutions. This process of creative destruction is a hallmark of a thriving capitalist economy, as it continually pushes the boundaries of what is possible and drives progress forward, and we need to embrace it. Entrepreneurs who are willing to take on the challenge of building a "better mousetrap" are the lifeblood of the capitalist system. They are the ones who see opportunities where others see obstacles and who are willing to invest their time, energy, and resources into turning their ideas into reality. By doing so, they not only create value for themselves and their investors but also contribute to the overall economic well-being of their communities and the nation.

Entrepreneurship in Urban Areas

One of the key challenges facing the capitalist system is the naturally occurring but many times uneven distribution of economic opportunity and prosperity. Many urban areas, particularly those with **high crime rates, poor infrastructure, and social instability**, have struggled to foster a vibrant entrepreneurial ecosystem. Addressing this issue is crucial for ensuring that all segments of the population feel the benefits of capitalism. The method to improve the ecosystem is where C.F.S.M communism is most damaging. It all comes back to the "free rider" concepts that we've discussed previously, but in its simplest form, to succeed, it is teaching that individual to fish and to feel comfortable with fishing in a lake that isn't made of lava.

To encourage entrepreneurship in these underserved areas, a multi-pronged approach is necessary. The first and most critical step is to address issues of **crime and public safety**. When individuals and families feel secure in their environment, they are more likely to plant roots and take the risks associated with starting a new business. Starting a business is tough enough, even without the added stress of crime. Imagine pouring your heart and soul into building something, only to have it destroyed by a crime spree overnight. It's a risk most people aren't willing to take. That's why tackling crime and restoring order in these communities is so important. It's about creating an environment where businesses can thrive, not just survive. We see it all the time on the news – boarded-up stores, empty storefronts – it's a clear sign that crime is driving away investment and opportunity and the family.

Many of these devastated urban areas are the ongoing result of the failed "Great Society" programs. To paraphrase the late Prime Minister of Great Britain, Margaret Thatcher, "Socialism is great until you run out of other people's money," and we are out of free money.

Once we've laid the groundwork for safety and education, we can start providing resources like capital, mentorship, and support to help small businesses grow. But simply throwing money at businesses in crime-ridden areas isn't the answer. It's very risky for both the lender and the borrower – the businesses will fail, and the borrower will be left with a lot of debt. This isn't about socialism; it's about creating a system where businesses have a real chance to succeed in creating real generational wealth, not just a handout with no accountability.

So, once safety and improved education are established, the creation of targeted investment funds, the development of incubator and accelerator programs, and the fostering of partnerships between established businesses and budding entrepreneurs can begin to occur. By empowering families and individuals in these urban areas to pursue their entrepreneurial dreams, we can not only drive economic growth but also foster a sense of community pride and self-reliance. This, in turn, can have a ripple effect, inspiring future generations to follow in the footsteps of these successful entrepreneurs and further strengthening the foundations of the capitalist system and our urban communities and, most importantly, getting away from these failed C.F.S.M communist plans.

Are Any Opportunities Left?

The American story is replete with examples of individuals who have taken the entrepreneurial leap and achieved remarkable success. An ever-growing GDP (gross domestic product) serves as a powerful reminder of the transformative potential of capitalism and the rewards that come with hard work, innovation, and a willingness to take risks.

One such example is the story of Elon Musk, the visionary behind companies like Tesla and SpaceX. Musk's journey epitomizes the American entrepreneurial spirit, as he has continually reinvested and risked his profits into bigger and more ambitious projects, pushing the boundaries of what is possible in the realms of electric vehicles, renewable energy, and space exploration. Despite facing numerous setbacks and challenges along the way, Musk's perseverance and unwavering commitment to his vision have made him a living embodiment of the American Dream. Another inspiring family tale is that of Donald Trump, whose father started the family business in real estate, which provided him with a solid foundation to build a multibillion-dollar empire. Trump's ability to identify opportunities, take calculated risks, and leverage his resources to expand his enterprise serves as a testament to the power of entrepreneurship and the creation of generational wealth and charity to spur opportunity.

These family stories, and countless others like them, show the power of capitalism to transform lives and communities through families. By showcasing successful entrepreneurs, we inspire others to take risks, innovate, and build something great. It's about celebrating those who contribute to our nation's economic strength. We should never demonize success, especially when entrepreneurs create so many jobs and opportunities. **But when truly successful people turn around and advocate for socialism, it sends a confusing message to families.** It's a contradiction that undermines the very system that allowed them to achieve their success.

The disingenuous nature of these C.F.S.M socialists and former capitalists can be misleading at first glance. However, a deeper examination reveals a consistent pattern: a pursuit of increased power and consolidation of their own positions of influence. These individuals, often wielding significant wealth and influence, are not true capitalists but rather utilize the capitalist system for personal gain, which only can't halt their tyrannical ambitions. Their actions are fundamentally antithetical to the principles of moral free markets and individual liberty.

Their interventions in various sectors, often driven by a monopolistic mindset, aim to restrict both freedom and choice for the broader population. Their actions, while appearing philanthropic on the surface, ultimately serve to erode individual agency and undermine the very fabric of a free society.

An entire book can be written on this topic but suffice it to say that they are also antithetical to family stability.

Economics, The Family and "Climate Change"

The ongoing debate surrounding "climate change" and the appropriate policy responses to address this global challenge has significant implications for the future of our economic system and all global families. As governments and policymakers grapple with the complex trade-offs between environmental protection and economic growth, it is crucial that these decisions are informed by a comprehensive understanding of the underlying issues and the potential regulatory consequences that all families face.

At the heart of the climate change discussion is the question of the primary drivers of this phenomenon. While the "politically accepted" scientific consensus claims that humans are the main driving factors for greenhouse gas emissions and other planetary changes, there are also very compelling arguments that suggest natural climate cycles and solar activity play a more significant role, as evidenced in the book 'Dark Winter' By John Casey. Casey's premise is very compelling, and the data that he shows significantly backs up his claims that the changes in our planetary climate are due to cycles that germinate from the sun's solar patterns and not man. Specifically, every 206 years represents a cycle, and we are at the tail end and beginning of a new cycle.

On its face, this is extremely logical, as all suns have a lifetime and cycle through patterns. This isn't to say that pollution isn't a problem, as it is and always will be, as humans are generally takers from the environment; however, directing resources and blaming humans for everything takes away from resources in another area that can be used to better the human condition and support families.

The complexity of the climate system and the inherent uncertainties involved in modeling and predicting long-term trends make this a highly contentious issue. It is not the focus of this book, but it has to be addressed as families bear the brunt of the policy consequences.

The resulting policy responses proposed by various stakeholders, from government officials to environmental activists, often diverge widely and hysterically, thus reflecting the underlying ideological differences and competing priorities that shape the climate change debate and are at the heart of the human fight for Freedom over Communism.

Resource Allocation And "Climate Change"

Regardless of the specific causes of climate change, the supposed political need to address its potential impacts presents significant **resource allocation** challenges for U.S. policymakers and the broader economic system and directly affects the lower half of the U.S. and global populations negatively from an economic perspective.

Better decisions must be made regarding the appropriate balance between environmental protection, economic growth, and the well-being of individual families and communities. This again plays directly into the hands of the elite, compelling their C.F.S.M socialistic wills over the lower half of the population, directly impacting families and individuals in every country, and disproportionately taking resources from the United States families to achieve C.F.S.M socialistic agendas. This is one of the main reasons why we advocate for all politicians to have a minimum of five, preferably 10 years of private sector experience before entering public office. It is so that they have a better understanding of what it is like for the public versus the career politician who becomes part of the C.F.S.M communist system at a very young age.

These trade-offs are often framed in terms of "**resource allocation**" and "**opportunity cost**." The finite nature of any global resources, such as oil, natural gas, water, minerals, and land, necessitates careful consideration of how these resources should be utilized to maximize family benefit first, then societal and finally global economic benefits. However, we argue that if you satisfy family needs and empower the family, the rest will take care of itself. We often hear that Americans should shoulder the burden of global initiatives like the Paris Accords. This is flawed thinking, as the agreement is not constitutionally binding and has not been ratified by the Senate. Instead, we should focus on strengthening the family unit, the foundation of a strong society. Families who own property are more likely to invest in its sustainable development, balancing profit with environmental responsibility in a moral way. Overregulation stifles families and has far-reaching negative consequences. It's about empowering families, not burdening them with unnecessary restrictions and over-taxation without true representation.

It's important to consider the **opportunity cost (what could have been done with the money)** of investing in restrictive climate mitigation strategies. While climate change is a serious "fake concern" to modern C.F.S.M communists, we need to weigh those investments against other crucial priorities like business formation, healthcare, education, food, energy costs and infrastructure, all of which directly impact families first and foremost. It's about finding a balance that supports both environmental sustainability and the well-being of families and removing tyranny from the equation.

Batteries vs. Hydrogen

As the climate change debate continues, the search for sustainable energy solutions has become a critical priority. One promising avenue is the development of hydrogen-based technologies, which hold the potential to provide a clean, abundant, and cost-effective energy source for the future.

Of course, we still have natural gas and nuclear energy, which are both very clean burning. However, in the U.S., we are often influenced by the Al Gore "I invented the Internet" and "all the polar bears are dying" (both false) hysteria when it comes to **man-made** climate change. Now, the new argument comes down to batteries as an energy source or hydrogen, and by far, hydrogen is the long-term winner.

Hydrogen (H) is the most abundant element in the universe and has the potential to power not only our planet but also our exploration of the cosmos. Unlike fossil fuels or lithium-ion batteries, which rely on finite resources and often involve environmentally damaging extraction processes, hydrogen-based systems offer a path toward greater energy independence and environmental sustainability.

It is important to note that there are several forms of hydrogen energy, each denoted by different colors such as gray, blue, green, yellow, turquoise, and pink. Each form has a different composition with hydrogen, and some are cleaner than others. Batteries contain heavy metals, have fire safety issues, and various toxic chemicals, and can leach into the groundwater supply system, thus leading to contamination. In addition to these harmful environmental effects, they also have limited power and rely on fossil fuel-generated power for charging. While I understand the benefits, I don't believe they are long-term suitable for our planet. Our planet needs the abundant element hydrogen, which can be used with combustible engines and be supplied to gas stations with only minor modifications. It is much more environmentally friendly in terms of pollution, and we will never run out of it.

Earlier, we talked about fiscal and monetary policy. Now, let's focus on a strong fiscal policy that prioritizes investment in hydrogen-powered energy. The US should lead the way in this area, as it has the potential to revolutionize industries and upgrade our power grid. It's a bold move that could create millions of good jobs, reduce our reliance on fossil fuels, and put us at the forefront of a clean energy future without raping the planet or hurting families through EV mandates.

The economic implications of a successful transition to hydrogen-powered technology are significant. By reducing the costs of energy production and distribution, we can create a more favorable environment for economic growth and prosperity. The lower energy prices that would result from widespread hydrogen adoption would have a very positive ripple effect, reducing the costs of transportation, manufacturing, and a wide range of other goods and services. This, in turn, would help to keep inflation in check, ensuring that the purchasing power of families is not eroded by rising prices and lead us into a global economic revolution. Furthermore, the shift towards hydrogen will open new avenues for entrepreneurship and innovation as individuals and businesses seek to develop and commercialize the technologies that will power the next generation of economic activity.

Safe hydrogen power allows for the development of powerful combustion engines in our automobiles and our planes while maintaining the infrastructure of many industries, such as gas stations, automobile plants, and aircraft development facilities. Hydrogen burns clean; we will never run out of it, and it checks all the environmental boxes. Why are we not pursuing this more aggressively?

It is important to note that this is not to dismiss the potential role of other renewable energy sources, such as solar and wind power, which have their own important contributions to make.

Rather, the argument is that hydrogen, with its unique properties and abundance, offers a particularly promising path forward in the quest for sustainable energy solutions that can support continued economic growth and development and directly contribute to the wealth and development of stable families, which, of course, contributes to stable governments. Low-cost energy that is clean and abundant is the key to planetary peace as it directly benefits the world's lower-income areas and takes away positions of power from the elite. Hydrogen should lead the way as it occurs naturally in the atmosphere and, therefore, can take the place of other existing energy sources with none of the drawbacks.

Balancing Families Against Government Climate Regulations

The debate surrounding climate change and the appropriate policy responses highlights the inherent tension between environmental protection and family economic priorities. The economic well-being of families and communities must be considered first.

Policies that focus solely on environmental goals can have significant negative consequences for employment, consumer prices, and overall standards of living, potentially leading to human conflict. It's important to ask: what's the point of restrictive climate policies if they negatively impact individuals and families to the extent that they cause consternation and suffering, potentially leading to conflicts or even wars? While avoiding war is a universal goal, if our freedom and security are at risk, the probability of conflict increases.

The challenge, then, is to find a balanced approach that addresses environmental concerns while also preserving and promoting economic prosperity and the freedom of families and individuals. This requires a nuanced understanding of the underlying issues, the potential trade-offs involved, and the ways in which innovative technologies and market-based solutions, coupled with private property ownership, can be leveraged to achieve both environmental sustainability and economic growth. One key aspect of this balancing act is the need to avoid the temptation of heavy-handed government intervention or the imposition of arbitrary targets and mandates. History has shown that when governments attempt to dictate resource allocation and production decisions based on political ideology rather than market forces and scientific evidence, the results are often disastrous, as evidenced by numerous historical examples.

Instead, the focus should be on creating a policy environment that **incentivizes** private-sector innovation, entrepreneurship, and the development of new technologies like Hydrogen (H) fuel that can address environmental challenges while also supporting economic growth.

This involves the removal of regulatory barriers and enhances the strategic investment in research and development, both of which can help to align the interests of environmental protection and economic prosperity.

Ultimately, the goal should be to empower families and strengthen communities to make informed choices about their energy use, consumption patterns, educational priorities and investment decisions, rather than having these choices dictated to them by government edict and by unelected C.F.S.M bureaucrats.

By fostering a culture of personal responsibility, family-centric innovation, and market-based solutions, we can navigate the complex terrain of climate change and economic policy in a way that strengthens the foundations of the capitalist system and secures a prosperous future for generations to come. A deeper understanding of economic principles and the capitalist system is of paramount importance in the current political and social landscape for us all. The lack of economic knowledge among our elected leaders and the public presents a significant threat to the continued prosperity and growth of the United States.

We can cultivate a new generation of free citizens who are equipped to navigate the complexities of the free market system, make informed decisions, and contribute to the economic well-being of their families and communities and, thus, make America an even better place to live and flourish.

This is what is at the core of the true MAGA movement, formerly the Tea Party Movement. MAGA isn't a harking back to a time and place of supposed happiness but is a quest for future fairness and peace of mind through morally stable families and opportunity. That isn't always conveyed properly and is often misunderstood and demonized as it has freedom and choice at its core. This is the reason it is extremely popular among most family units as a whole.

At the core of this effort is the recognition that the individual in the family unit is the foundational building block of a thriving capitalist society. By empowering parents to choose education to better understand and utilize the principles of capitalism, we can cement the role of choice and individual contribution, which will impact economic policies and strengthen the foundations of our economic system to ensure its continued success and end the C.F.S.M communist influence. The entrepreneurial spirit, with its willingness to take risks and drive innovation, is the engine that propels economic growth and progress. By celebrating the success stories of entrepreneurs, both native-born and immigrant, and creating an environment that fosters entrepreneurial activity, particularly in underserved, unsafe urban areas, we can unlock the full potential of the capitalist system and ensure that its benefits are enjoyed by all segments of the population.

As we navigate the complex and often contentious debate surrounding climate change, it is crucial that we approach these issues with a clear-eyed understanding of the economic implications and the need to strike a balance between environmental protection and economic prosperity. By embracing the potential of new energy technologies, such as hydrogen, and fostering market-based solutions, we can chart a path forward that addresses environmental concerns while also supporting the continued growth and development of the capitalist system without having a severe impact on family's economic decisions.

Ultimately, the path to economic prosperity and stability lies in empowering individuals, families, and, subsequently, communities to become active contributors to the system rather than passive consumers or "free riders." By instilling the principles of capitalism, encouraging entrepreneurship, and fostering a culture of personal responsibility, morality and civic engagement without impacting the concepts of freedom and choice, we can ensure that the United States continues to be a beacon of economic opportunity and a testament to the transformative power of the free market system.

Chapter 7: United States 12.0 – Elimination of C.F.S.M by Empowering Parents and Family

The United States has long been hailed as a beacon of freedom and prosperity, drawing inspiration from the legacies of great civilizations that came before it. However, the parallels between the trajectory of the United States and that of the Roman Empire cannot be ignored. Just as the Roman Empire went through cycles of adaptation and decline, the United States now finds itself at a critical juncture, facing challenges that threaten to undermine the very foundations upon which it was built.

At the heart of this crisis lies the erosion of the family unit – the fundamental building block of a stable and thriving society. The MAGA (Make America Great Again) movement, with its emphasis on restoring family values, recognizes the vital role that parents and families play in shaping the future of the nation. By empowering parents and strengthening the family unit, we can address the underlying issues plaguing the United States and embark on a path toward lasting stability and prosperity and eliminating Communism and Marxism influence.

In this final chapter, we will explore the lessons of the Roman Empire, analyze the current challenges facing the United States, and outline a comprehensive strategy to stabilize the nation through the empowerment of parents and families. This is the blueprint for America 12.0 – a vision of a revitalized, resilient, and expansive United States that can serve as a beacon of hope for the world by demonstrating that we bend, but we don't break.

The Roman Empire's Cycles of Adaptation and Decline

The rise and fall of the Roman Empire serve as a powerful cautionary tale for the United States.

While the two nations share certain structural and philosophical similarities, the Roman Empire's reliance on military conquest and coercive power ultimately tested the empire's ability to manage such gains and realized it could not, and it ultimately was a major cause that led to its downfall. Conversely, the United States has historically been centered on the principles of individual and religious freedom and the dignity of the citizen first and all else second, and fiercely fought to defend those values.

In the early days of the Roman Republic, the system of government bore a striking resemblance to that of the United States, with a senior and junior council akin to the president and vice president and a legislative body with similarities to the modern-day Congress. However, as the Roman Empire expanded through military might, the quest for power gradually eroded the republic's foundations and ability to control it all, and thus, after Caesar's assassination, the age of Emperors was born. Are we at a similar point?

UNITED STATES 12.0 – FREEDOM VS. COMMUNISM

One of the early pivotal moments in the Roman Empire's history was the three Punic Wars, where young Rome suffered a devastating battle loss to the Carthaginian general Hannibal and others. Yet, rather than succumbing to defeat, Rome displayed a remarkable ability to learn from its mistakes and adapt and ultimately won all three wars. Hannibal, who it was thought could have easily conquered Rome, chose to halt his advance and not fully conquer Rome.

He eventually lost the 2nd Punic War, and then Rome destroyed Carthage in 146 BCE in the 3rd and final war; Rome became the world's new superpower, and through military might, it never looked back.

This pattern of learning from setbacks and continuously evolving would become a hallmark of the Roman Empire. As new generals and military leaders rose to prominence, Rome became an increasingly powerful entity, driven by its relentless pursuit of conquest and territorial expansion and producing one solid military leader after another, each anxious to outshine their counterparts and all from the upper echelon of Roman society.

Rome fell for many reasons; however, this quest for power and wealth for territorial gains put governance and commitment to the test and ultimately contributed to the downfall of the Roman Empire. The corruption and overreach of numerous influential figures gradually eroded the foundations of the Roman Republic over time. While some notable individuals like Julius Caesar were thought to be ruthlessly tyrannical, Rome did live in a time when the only thing the world respected was power, and their system lasted on the low end 500 and high 1,000 years, depending on counting. We are much younger, and the world is still on fire.

The Roman Empire's eventual collapse and split into two at the hands of the Visigoths in 410 A.D. marked the end of a stable but militaristic era. The Dark Ages that ensued serve as a sobering reminder of the fragility of even the greatest civilizations, as it took over 1,000 years of human suffering before the Age of Enlightenment was born, which we count starting when Christopher Columbus discovered America in 1492...America 1.0.

Yet, the legacy of Rome lives on, most notably through the widespread adoption of Christianity, which became a stabilizing force within the empire and the globe, as the religious concepts of brotherhood and love cemented in morality were somewhat antithetical to what drove Roman conquest.

As the United States contemplates its own trajectory, the lessons of the Roman Empire loom large. The numerous changes and adaptations that the Roman Empire underwent, driven by both military conquests and losses, are a testament to the dynamic nature of great powers. The United States, too, has faced its own share of challenges and must be willing to learn from its mistakes and evolve accordingly. To date, we have made it through some incredibly tumultuous times. However, should the U.S. fall, the power vacuum will clearly go to Communist China, and the new era of the Dark

Ages will commence. The key difference between Rome and the U.S. lies in the philosophical underpinnings of the two nations. While the Roman Empire relied on military might and coercion, the United States has historically been built upon the moral principles of individual freedom, the rule of law, and the dignity of the citizen. It is this moral foundation that must be strengthened and safeguarded as the United States navigates the path toward stabilization and prosperity.

Why does the C.F.S.M Communist hate MAGA so much?

As the United States grapples with the complexities of the modern era, it finds itself confronted with a myriad of issues that threaten to undermine the very fabric of the nation. At the heart of this crisis is the erosion of the family unit – the bedrock upon which a thriving society is built.

The MAGA movement, with its rallying cry of "Make America Great Again," resonates with a deep-seated desire to restore the values and principles that have made the United States a beacon of hope for the world through the family unit. However, the true essence of MAGA lies not in nostalgia for a bygone era, which is what its detractors don't get.

As stated, it is the recognition that the stability and prosperity of the nation are inextricably linked to the strength, safety and resilience of the family unit. That is what MAGA means more than anything else, as all the changes that are needed are necessary to make the family unit strong again and, in turn, the country. Maslow's hierarchy of needs provides a useful framework for understanding the challenges facing the United States. At the base of the pyramid, the need for security – both physical and emotional – must be addressed. Without a sense of safety and stability, individuals and families cannot meaningfully progress towards higher-level needs such as self-actualization and fulfillment.

The destabilization and ultimate destruction of the family unit have created a growing void at the very foundation of American society. As parents and families struggle to navigate the complexities of modern life, they are beset by a host of challenges that undermine their ability to provide a stable and nurturing environment for their children.

These challenges, all previously stated, include, but are not limited to, the ongoing crisis at the southern border, the erosion of media integrity, the rampant spread of media misinformation and outright propaganda, the lack of election integrity, the rise in crime, the breakdown of the rule of law, the bloated and inefficient federal bureaucracy, and the failings of the education system.

Each of these issues, compounded with the threat of financial collapse due to mounting federal debt, has the potential to further destabilize the family and, by extension, the entire nation. This dynamic mirrors how Rome fell, except it's going to be at a much faster rate due to the speed of information and mob control through social media. This is the goal of the C.F.S.M communists. To collapse our Constitutional Republic with crushing debt, creating only two classes and controlling us for as long as they can.

Addressing these challenges will require a multi-pronged approach that prioritizes the empowerment of parents and the strengthening of the family unit to a level that we have never seen before. By securing the moral and financial foundation of the family, we can create a stable base from which the United States can embark on a path toward lasting prosperity and stability, and that is what the C.F.S.M communist hates the most.

Reviewing the Path to U.S. 12.0

The key to stabilizing the tumultuous United States and achieving the vision of America 12.0 lies in the empowerment of parents and the revitalization of the family unit. By addressing the core issues that undermine the strength and resilience of families, we can create a solid foundation upon which the nation can thrive.

Educational Choice that will lead to Reform

One of the most critical areas in need of reform is the education system, which is nothing short of horrendous. The current educational model, which was designed with the intent of creating obedient citizens rather than entrepreneurial thinkers, has failed to keep pace with the evolving needs of the 21st century, and the model needs to be blown up. The United States, once a global leader in education, has been steadily losing ground at all levels, with pre-college, post-college, and even college-level performance declining at a rapid pace. This is a clear indication that the system is in dire need of transformation.

The concept of educational **choice** is a powerful tool in the parent revolution to stabilize the family unit. Empowering parents to have a direct say in the education of their children by allowing them to choose ANY school they wish will clean up the system.

We can create an efficient and responsive system that better serves the needs of families by allowing parents to use up to 75% of all education dollars to choose where and how they wish to educate their child… private, public, online, AI, tutors… on and on. The bloated C.F.S.M bureaucracies coupled with public teacher unions will instantly suffer a massive defeat as parents know what is in the best interests of their children far better than any administrator or teacher ever will. This change is at the heart of choice.

This decentralized choice-based approach has real teeth in that efficiencies will take place through a positive reward process as parents will demand better education across the board as they now hold the power…NOT THE GOVERNMENT or UNIONS!

Additional reforms will begin to take place involving shorter school days but longer time periods, with a greater emphasis on internship-style activities and social engagement to foster competition and respect for others. This approach would help break the cycle of constant cell phone usage, which has been a significant contributor to the anxiety and mental health challenges facing millions of children. The positive effects of engaged moral children who have trusted relationships will grow and have a positive ripple effect the size of a tidal wave. At the same time, we will be able to identify the lost individuals who seek connection and purpose quickly and hopefully reduce the dastardly shootings and the like.

Additionally, by giving parents control over the purse strings of their educational dollars, we can incentivize the creation of better teachers through payments for performance, reduce the bloated C.F.S.M bureaucracy of administrators, and foster an entrepreneurial mindset among students and institutions. This shift in the balance of power will transform the educational system without the need for extensive top-down reforms as parents will guide the process through financial empowerment and ease of changing schools at will.

The level of opposition to this one proposal is so intense as it attacks the core of Communism, Fascism, Socialism and Marxism, which all seek to take your children from you and make them perpetual pawns of the State. This must happen if the family unit is to survive.

Economic Incentives for Family Units

The financial stability outside of education of families is another critical aspect that must be addressed to empower parents and strengthen the family unit. The erosion of the job market, with companies increasingly outsourcing and going overseas, has made it increasingly difficult for families to maintain a sense of financial security.

The idea of a single-earner household, where one parent can stay at home to help rear children and make important decisions, has become a rarity in modern America. Instead, both parents are often forced to work, leading to a fragmentation of the family unit and a diminished ability to provide the necessary support and guidance to their children. There is no substitute for time with your children, now more than ever.

To combat this trend, policymakers must explore creative financial incentives that incentivize family units to stay together by **replacing child tax credits and implementing broader support for nuclear and extended families via the tax structure to create real wealth.** Allowing families to create wealth through low taxes and business creation will greatly appeal to families and create the initial formation of generational wealth.

It's important to understand that completely removing the child tax credit would significantly impact the financial stability of many split families. What we really need to focus on is advocating for a tax and small business structure that is family-friendly and also able to generate real wealth. This is the conversation that our representatives immediately need to have. Addressing the healthcare needs of seniors and extended families is a critical component of the family unit that has been largely neglected, but suffice it to say that making it financially easier to care for loved ones as they advance in age will also have very positive effects and help families stay together.

By providing families with the economic resources and stability they need, we can empower parents to focus on their most important role: nurturing and guiding their children. This, in turn, will strengthen communities, bolster public and private schools, and ultimately contribute to the overall prosperity of the nation.

Strengthening Of Communities

The empowerment of parents and families has a ripple effect that extends far beyond the individual household. As families become more secure, stable, and engaged, the communities in which they reside will also experience a resurgence of strength and vitality.

This community-level transformation, which admittedly mostly begins at the school level, is essential for the long-term stability of the United States. Strong, cohesive and engaged communities provide a critical support system for families, offering resources, opportunities, and a sense of shared responsibility. When families are financially liberated and thriving, the communities in which they live will naturally become more vibrant and resilient.

It is important to remember that at the core of this community-level transformation is the concept of consumption. Families, as the key drivers of consumption, are the lifeblood of the United States' economic engine. By fostering an environment that supports and empowers families financially through choice, we can unlock the full potential of every family, and this will improve the nation's GDP growth and create a "bigger pie" for us all.

However, the path to strengthening communities and empowering families is not without its challenges. The current climate of victimization and the divisive tactics employed by C.F.S.M communist ideologies pose a significant threat to the unity and resilience of American communities.

The C.F.S.M communist approach, rooted in creating victims across various demographics, is fundamentally at odds with the values of individual achievement, personal dignity, and the freedom of choice that are the hallmarks of both Capitalism and the United States. By breaking free from this "victimization mindset" and embracing a vision of shared prosperity through healthy competition, we can cultivate communities that are truly unified and resilient.

Martin Luther King's "I Have a Dream" speech is relevant here and today more than ever. And it isn't just relevant to black citizens; it is relevant to us all. The central theme of the speech identifies the faults of America and the importance of everyone being treated equally regardless of their background.

Communists use bureaucratic power to enforce their will, which is why all of the power of bureaucrats must be diminished dramatically and swiftly. C.F.S.M Communists seek to divide us, and they begin with the family unit. They pit mothers against fathers and children against parents, all with the hope that the government is the savior. The world is filled with constant evil examples of this failed ideology, and it requires each and every one of us to take action to stomp and flush out this concept of victimization and reject it across the board.

Foundational Challenges

To achieve the stabilization of the United States and the realization of America 12.0, we must address a series of foundational challenges that have undermined the strength and integrity of the nation.

We must stop the bleeding before we can repair anything, and to do that, we must address these challenges. These challenges include but are not limited to the ongoing illegal immigration crisis, the massive educational problem, the lack of media integrity, the loss of personal freedoms right now, the erosion of election integrity, the rise in crime and the breakdown of the rule of law, and the bloated and inefficient federal bureaucracy.

1. Immigration and Border Security

The invasion of the United States across our borders must be stopped immediately. Deportations of criminal elements must commence without delay, and the concept of American citizenship must be reborn. Just as a Roman citizen once commanded respect and deterrence in the most hostile of territories, the idea of American citizenship must be imbued with a sense of dignity and inviolability.

2. Educational Choice –

Parents and families must be able to choose the school they send their child to and or how their child is educated, and they must command the dollars to do so.

3. Honesty and Integrity in the Media

The media landscape has become a battleground of misinformation and censorship, eroding the public's trust in the very institutions that are meant to inform and enlighten. The ability of parents to hold social media companies accountable and to curate the content that their children are exposed to must be a top priority. Corporate ownership of these entities must cease.

4. Election & Politician Integrity and Simplicity

Fair and honest elections are the cornerstone of a functioning constitutional republic. The implementation of measures such as photo ID requirements, fingerprint on ballots as a check, the elimination of mail-in ballots, and the establishment of a federal holiday for voting are essential steps in restoring the integrity of the electoral process.

To restore this integrity, we also must remove corporate dollars from this process and focus again on local debates and policy. It shouldn't cost $2 billion to run for the presidency as the job itself only pays $400,000 a year. We must completely get away from the career politician and establish **term qualifications,** not term limits. Anyone seeking public office should have at least five to 10 years of private sector exposure and experience, with 10 being the preference. This alone would do away with the career politician, which is something we all seek. Nobody wants another 50-year politician like Joe Biden with little to no record of accomplishment other than Self-aggrandizement.

5. Crime, Activist Judges and the Rule of Law

The rise in crime and the breakdown of the rule of law pose a direct threat to the security and stability of families and communities. Removing rogue prosecutors and activist judges who refuse to prosecute and punish crimes. Reestablishing the primacy of the Constitution as the guiding principle of the legal system is crucial for restoring faith in the justice system. If we don't have faith in our legal system, the concept of fear will spread like wildfire, which it has already, and it will lead to numerous negative externalities and create a climate where the human soul is suppressed. The innocent must be protected, the criminals must be punished, and the righteous must be set free to achieve and strive.

6. Reducing the Size and Scope of the Federal Bureaucracy

The bloated and inefficient federal bureaucracy, which has become a breeding ground for communist and socialist ideologies, must be drastically reduced in size and scope. By freezing personnel and wages for a ten-year period and allowing for the natural migration of workers from the public to the private sector, we can streamline the government and redirect resources toward more productive and growth-oriented initiatives.

It is important to note that without the private sector, the government would cease to exist. This may seem simplistic, but because we keep gravitating more and more towards a C.F.S.M socialist model, people don't understand the simplicity of that statement, which goes hand in hand with one of the reasons for writing this book. In its simplest form, people are worried that Social Security won't be there for them when they get older, and that may very well happen due to the spending and financial complexities that exist due to massive debt.

The United States must stop all world aid until we rectify our debt issues. We must fix our debt problems and become stronger by M.A.G.A through financially empowering middle-class families and all families.

Addressing these foundational challenges is essential for creating the stable and secure environment that families and communities need to thrive. By tackling these issues head-on, we can lay the groundwork for the realization of America 12.0 – a vision of a prosperous, resilient, and expansive United States that can serve as a beacon of hope for the world.

The Vision of America 12.0 and Beyond

With the empowerment of parents and families at the core of our strategy, the path to achieving the vision of America 12.0 becomes clear. As we address the foundational challenges and create an environment that fosters the strength and resilience of the family unit, the United States will once again become the "shining city on a hill" – a beacon of hope and prosperity for the world, as Ronald Regan stated numerous times.

The stabilization of the United States through the empowerment of parents and families will have far-reaching consequences, both domestically and globally. As the nation regains its footing and reclaims its moral position as a global leader of human rights, other countries facing similar challenges will be inspired to follow suit, adopting the principles and practices that have made the United States a bastion of freedom and opportunity.

This positive, **voluntary** emulation of the American model, rather than the forced imposition of communist or Marxist ideologies, like what is trying to be done with Taiwan by China, will naturally lead to a reduction in the influx of illegal immigrants seeking a better life in the United States. As other nations embrace the values of individual dignity, the rule of law, and the strength of the family unit, they, too, will become more prosperous and stable, reducing the incentive for their citizens to seek a better life elsewhere. **These are the countries the U.S.... should provide financial aid to IF, and only IF should they commit to our**

constitutional principles. The entire concept of financial aid must change to support our freedom-based way of life. Do note that it is up to the individual citizens of each respective country to force their government to strive for these basic human rights changes and to emulate our example once or IF we stabilize… again.

Moreover, the United States should remain **open to the incorporation of new states**, welcoming the moral cultures and perspectives of other nations and strengthening the diversity that has long been a source of our nation's vitality. By respecting the cultures of other countries and integrating them into the fabric of the United States, we can create a culture of shared prosperity and understanding, but only if they **fully embrace the model** that we demonstrate AND make it work. A simple test would be when zero people want to migrate to the U.S. This would be one solid indicator that the country is ready for U.S. statehood.

That's why the invasion that is taking place must be fully reversed and by force if necessary since it is OUR family structure and OUR constitutional fabric that is most at risk, as now our entire country is at risk. We must be protected to survive. If we are truly a nation of laws, any new entrant must begin by following our laws.

Looking beyond America 12.0, the vision for the United States 13.0 is one of true expansion – not just within the confines of our borders but into the vast expanse of space. The exploration of the cosmos, the pursuit of scientific discovery, and the realization of the human potential to venture beyond our earthly confines represent the next frontier for the United States. However, this vision of a prosperous and expansive United States 13.0 can only be achieved if we act now to embrace 12.0. We all study history to avoid repeating mistakes of the past, and so the lessons of the Roman Empire serve as a sobering reminder that even the greatest civilizations are not immune to decline. **Globalist forces of Communism, Fascism, Socialism, and Marxism always lurk in the shadows, ready to plunge the world into a new Dark Age should we fail to heed the warnings of history.**

Globalism should take place, but it should be U.S. Globalism leading the way, as our system is just better across the board.

It is time for us, especially our children, to learn from the evils of the past and to empower parents and families with the tools they need to stabilize the foundation of our society. By doing so, we can ensure that the United States remains a beacon of hope and prosperity, not just for our own citizens but for generations to come. The path to America 12.0 and beyond is clear, and the time to act is now.

The stabilization of the United States through the leadership of parents and families is not just a lofty goal but a necessity for the long-term prosperity and security of the nation. As we grapple with the challenges of the modern era, we must draw upon the lessons of history and the enduring strength of the family unit to chart a course toward a brighter future. The MAGA movement, with its focus on restoring family integrity and values, recognizes the central role that parents and families play in shaping the destiny of the United States. By addressing the foundational issues that threaten to undermine the stability of the family unit, we can create a solid foundation upon which the nation can thrive.

From educational choice and economic incentives to the strengthening of communities and the tackling of systemic challenges, the path to America 12.0 is a comprehensive and multifaceted endeavor. But it is one that must be undertaken with unwavering determination and a steadfast commitment to the principles that have made the United States the envy of the world.

As we look towards the future, the vision of the United States 13.0 – a nation that has not only stabilized its foundations but has also set its sights on the vast expanse of space – stands as a testament to the resilience and boundless potential of the American free spirit. But to reach this next frontier, we must first secure the stability of the family unit and the dignity and sanctity of the child.

The time to act is now. The lessons of the past have been laid bare, and the path forward is clear. Let us, as a nation, confront the challenges that threaten to undermine our stability and forge a future that will inspire generations to come. In doing so, we will not only make America great again, but we will ensure that the United States remains a shining beacon of hope and prosperity for all the world to see and emulate. What are you going to do now to help, because you can't sit on the sidelines anymore?